CONVENTIONAL IDIOCY

CONVENTIONAL IDIOCY

Why the New America Is Sick of Old Politics

Rick Sanchez

A CELEBRA BOOK

CELEBRA
Published by New American Library, a division of
Penguin Group (USA) Inc., 375 Hudson Street,
New York, New York 10014, USA
Penguin Group (Canada), 90 Eglinton Avenue East, Suite 700, Toronto,
Ontario M4P 2Y3, Canada (a division of Pearson Penguin Canada Inc.)
Penguin Books Ltd., 80 Strand, London WC2R 0RL, England
Penguin Ireland, 25 St. Stephen's Green, Dublin 2,
Ireland (a division of Penguin Books Ltd.)
Penguin Group (Australia), 250 Camberwell Road, Camberwell, Victoria 3124,
Australia (a division of Pearson Australia Group Pty. Ltd.)
Penguin Books India Pvt. Ltd., 11 Community Centre, Panchsheel Park,
New Delhi - 110 017, India
Penguin Group (NZ), 67 Apollo Drive, Rosedale, North Shore 0632,
New Zealand (a division of Pearson New Zealand Ltd.)
Penguin Books (South Africa) (Pty.) Ltd., 24 Sturdee Avenue,
Rosebank, Johannesburg 2196, South Africa

Penguin Books Ltd., Registered Offices:
80 Strand, London WC2R 0RL, England

First published by Celebra,
a division of Penguin Group (USA) Inc.

First Printing, September 2010
10 9 8 7 6 5 4 3 2 1

Copyright © Rick Sanchez, 2010
All rights reserved

CELEBRA and logo are trademarks of Penguin Group (USA) Inc.

Library of Congress Cataloging-in-Publication Data:

Sanchez, Rick.
  Conventional idiocy: why the new America is sick of old politics/Rick Sanchez.
    p. cm.
  ISBN 978-0-451-23139-0
  1. Political culture—United States. 2. United States—Politics and government—2009–
3. Political activists—Social networks—United States. 4. Political participation—United States. I. Title.
  JK1726.S322 2010
  306.20973—dc22   2010016064

Set in Minion
Designed by Ginger Legato

Printed in the United States of America

This book is dedicated to the hundreds of thousands of people on Twitter, Facebook and MySpace who believe that by connecting with one another, we can change the world for the better.

CONTENTS

CONVENTIONAL IDIOCY

INTRODUCTION

You Say
"They Don't Get Us!"

You say your money's being wasted! You say politicians—of all stripes—could give a crap about you! And you say that too often the media just puts you in a spin cycle hoping to keep you there long enough to collect. And what do you get? You get the shaft first of all, and then you get what you're supposed to accept as conventional wisdom. What is conventional wisdom? It's what we're told is generally believed by experts.

These experts are often just plain wrong. Conventional wisdom? You say that more often it's not wisdom at all, it's really more like conventional idiocy.

Who's to blame? The media, the politicians, the pundits, business leaders. Okay, they don't listen to you. I get it. And you know what? At least with some of them, I'm not sure they ever will listen.

Yes, Americans are sick of being spoon-fed the same old bogus conventional wisdom from so-called experts who don't listen to them. That's the overwhelming message I hear from you every single day. You're sick of the old ways, the old politics. You tell me you are skeptical, maybe more so than ever in our country's past, skeptical of government, skeptical of the media, skeptical of corporations. And you're showing your skepticism in polling data, on blogs, and—in the new way America connects—through social media.

You're tired of the BS. Little do they know that you're wide awake, you're engaged with what's going on in the country, and many of you are angry as hell.

Your anger, your concerns and frustrations, is what inspired me to write this book. From you I hear what is really on the minds of ordinary Americans, what you are thinking, what you are talking about, and above all what you're sick of—from the bankers who recklessly gambled with our money, to the politicians who play on our worst fears and prejudices, to the media demagogues who spread ignorance for ratings. In this book, I talk about all of that and more, and I draw from everything I've learned listening to you.

▓ Why Me?

Why do I know so much about what *you*'re sick of? It's because you tell me every minute of every day, through Twitter, MySpace, and Facebook. And I care about reporting what pisses *you* off. You've given me a responsibility to use my craft to give voice to our unsung heroes—*you!*

You say we've let the so-called conventional wisdom speak for America for too long and it's time for us, together, to respond—loud and unapologetically—with what we know is the truth, the unconventional truth!

Conventional Idiocy is more than a book; it's an extension of my life work as a broadcaster—to amplify your voice and frustrations. I do exactly that with my show, *Rick's List*, which is more of a national conversation than it is a news show. We don't just report the news, we listen to you and we talk to each other, through social media, and list your concerns while gathering the facts you need to know to better understand what's going on. Together we call people out and challenge the conventional wisdom. It's been hailed as "the next generation of news," because you the viewer have become an active participant in the "national conversation." Good for you; better yet, good for us. Twitter, Facebook, and MySpace have changed the way we communicate to each other. Now they are changing what we, together, communicate to the world.

In the conversation I have with you every day, you set the agenda, you drive the issues. It's *your* news; it's not what's decided for you in some ivory tower. It's not some out-of-touch pundit or politico lecturing you about what you should care about.

With *Conventional Idiocy*, I have taken this model from the show, this idea of a conversation, of listing your thoughts and what you need to know and applied it to a book. In that sense, it isn't even my book, it's your book. It's everything you tell me you're worried about, everything that bothers you about what's happening in our country, everything—and everyone—you're sick and tired of. In some cases, it's literally your voice—I have included in each chapter actual tweets from you.

My hope is that the book—driven as it is by you and by the concerns of everyday Americans—will cut through a lot of the BS that passes for political discourse today. America is speaking out, largely through social media, and saying it is sick of the old politics and the old ways.

It's this "conventional idiocy" that many of you want to change, to overturn, because you tell me that what passes for conventional wisdom is really about other people's interests, interests that aren't yours.

The Big Fat Lie

In my job I try to be—and this is what I believe most good CNN broadcasters attempt to be—engaged. I'm not an anchor who simply reads scripts or questions written by someone else. I don't feign curiosity, while reciting the words from a teleprompter as if I'm rehearsing an act for a high school musical. Too often that can turn into something you can see through like glass. It would be too easy to just read the questions prepared for me and then wait for the person I'm interviewing to answer with talking points handed to them by some PR flak or political group. You tell me you don't want that. That would be like a friggin' Fellini movie. I get it.

I could also play by the script. I could simply wait for the guest to finish talking, I wouldn't really need to listen to what he or she said, and then I'd read the next prewritten question. But that kind of journalism would be like dumb and dumber—and guess what? We all end up dumber for it, because we're expecting to hear something new or original. It isn't going to happen, folks!

Everyone has an off day, even at the network level, but I once worked with an anchor at the local level who took this theater of the bizarre to a whole different level. She was interviewing a state senator running for governor. She asked him how the race was going. He responded by giving her a huge scoop: He told her he was dropping out. When he said that, jaws immediately dropped in the control room, where producers were monitoring the live interview. The anchor, however, rather than follow up with a question about why he was dropping out, went on to ask her next prewritten question.

Like a trained seal, she read, "How do you think you'll do, what are your chances in the western part of the state?" while completely ignoring what he'd just said.

At this point the producer in the studio began yelling at her and trying to let her know the senator just said he was dropping out! The producer was yelling at her through her IFB, the interruptible fold back, which is a small rubber insert we wear in our ears that's connected to a wire to let us hear the broadcast and instructions from the control room.

As the anchor doing the live shoot began hearing the commotion, she got so flustered that she reached up and tried to adjust the volume by pulling on the rubber insert just enough to separate it from her ear. But with all the commotion and her jumpiness, she accidentally yanked on the wire and pulled the IFB out completely. Now she could hear nothing. Struggling to find something to say, she looked at the camera, then looked at the senator, then looked back at the camera and blurted out a line destined for TV blooper heaven.

"I'm sorry, Senator," she said, "I can't hear you, my IUD just fell out." She obviously meant to say IFB. An IUD is a contraceptive device that was very popular during the 1970s. Once inserted, it can keep you from getting pregnant, but it can't stop you from failing to listen to your guest and making a fool of yourself on television. Listening! What a concept.

It takes a gaffe like that for many of us to realize how important it is to listen. And it sends a message to you that on-air news gathering can sometimes look way too much like a Kabuki dance. What I'm learning from you is you want more. You tell me flat out . . .

Media does not give good info most time. Need more in depth analysis.

What's the key to more in-depth discussion from the news media? Listening. Listening is vital. Most of the media on the left and the right and the vast majority of politicians and corporate America have gotten so used to telling you what you ought to think that they've forgotten how to listen to you. They're so used to one-way communication that they're practically deaf. And because they can't listen, they can't hear.

You know that huge gap between the conventional wisdom about what Americans want to hear and what they *really* care about? Here, let me help you. This is what it sounds like: *Blah, blah,* and *blah.*

That's the sound of too many news conferences, TV news panels, newscasts, and political speeches. Their lips are moving, but I don't hear them saying anything. Background noise!

You want more than that, more than just background noise. This is what I hear from you. You're sick of it. You're *more* than sick of it. In the everlasting words of the fictional newscaster Howard Beale from the movie *Network*, you're mad as hell and you're not going to take it anymore.

Speaking of Howard Beale, let me tell you about one day while I was anchoring, when I decided to do my own version of Howard Beale. Strange TV bloopers happen when you least expect them and yes, I have my own version of one. I've often thought that cable news viewers watch us deliver the news as if we're, like I said earlier, background noise, or maybe elevator music: They barely pay attention. So this one day I decided to shake things up. I began the show by running out of the studio and screaming out the seventh-floor window of the Time Warner Center overlooking Central Park, "I'm mad as hell and I'm not going to take it anymore."

I was trying to make a point. It would have been very impactful and it really would have made my point about the confusion surrounding comprehensive immigration reform, if only the audio man had remembered to open my microphone.

Viewers saw me run out of the studio and scream, but they had no idea what I was saying. Oh well.

Okay, that was an extreme attempt to get viewers to pay attention. But really all it takes is something much simpler. Listening. Hearing from you, the American people, about the issues you genuinely care about. Having a conversation to bring these important issues out into the light—and then to challenge those in power who deny what Americans are really feeling and try to feed us the same old bull. That is what we've worked to develop with *Rick's List* and that is what this book is all about, too.

In the following chapters, I take you through a lot of behind-the-scenes moments from the show, where a guest has stated something that needed to be challenged and we—together, you and I and the CNN staff—have pointed out their inconsistencies. Some of the people I've had the most combative interviews with are people I respect, just as I respect my brothers, one of whom is very liberal and the other very conservative, or my friends with whom I disagree. In fact, that's the point of social media, the very concept I've tried to introduce into how I deliver the news. It's fresh, it's different, and it involves all of us finding common ground rather than relying on "conventional wisdom."

In many of these cases, the interviews went viral, receiving hundreds of thousands of hits on sites like YouTube.

That's because of you. And now, also because of you, a curious thing has started to happen. Many public figures and elected officials, on the left and the right, including many who've found themselves the targets of our criticisms and investigations in the past, have joined the conversation and are now actually tweeting me so that I can, in turn, share their comments and ideas with you. We hear from Senator John Mc-Cain and from the White House. We hear from Sarah Palin and Nancy Pelosi. We hear from Eric Cantor and from Bernie Sanders. And we hear from Shaquille O'Neal, and Britney Spears, and Reverend Al Sharpton; hey, everybody seems to want in. Yeah, it's working.

They began listening to me because they know I listen to you. Let me say that again: I got them to listen to me by listening to you. So now when they tweet/talk to me, I share it with you. It's that easy. They can't avoid hearing you. It's right there in their faces every day, through me and through you.

CNN President Jon Klein finally decided what we were doing every day at 3:00 p.m. was so different, and so impactful, that he expanded us to two hours and branded the show *Rick's List*. What he really did was give you a bigger voice.

Let me give you an example of how this works, of how together we hold someone's feet to the fire and make them accountable for their words.

▉ Eric Cantor's Conversion

When Republican whip Eric Cantor tweeted me in the middle of a newscast, suggesting that "prosperity" is threatened by "overregulation," antennas shot up around the country, including mine. Overregulation? Are you kidding me, Congressman? Don't you mean "under-regulation"?

With all the so-called scoundrels on Wall Street making out like bandits because laws were either passed or eliminated to suit them? With regulators looking the other way, being completely derelict in their duties and bringing us the closest we've ever come in this country to complete financial meltdown, you Congressman Cantor are *really* suggesting the problem is *over*regulation?

You told me to call him on it:

> Cantor couldn't be more wrong!!! If anything we
> need more laws and tighter enforcement.

> over reg? that's ridiculous.

And so I did. In that moment, I stopped my broadcast and instructed my booking producer—on the air (I knew Janelle Griffin would be watching the show)—"Get me Eric Cantor." I was challenging him on national television to explain himself. And the next day, to his credit, he did. He came on the show.

I pressed him and pressed him and eventually had to interrupt him (I know you say I sometimes interrupt too much, but I have to get your point across). My question was simple: Wasn't the problem under-regulation? He wouldn't say it. He simply wouldn't answer the question directly. Instead, he kept telling me how we can't take away "risk taking" and how Wall Street was "over-leveraged." He was giving me his talking points, his spin. God, I hate that.

Finally, well into the conversation, I asked him point-blank for about the third time if under-regulation caused the economic collapse. And finally, he was forced to admit it. The GOP whip told me on the record, contradicting his tweet, that "regulators did not do their jobs." Did you hear that, America? *Regulators did not do their jobs.*

That's under regulation. As the interview concluded, I asked him again just to be sure if he recognized that a lack of regulation caused the collapse. And guess what he did? He walked it back again, finishing with "I am for smarter regulation." The point is this: *You* recognize that we dropped the ball on Wall Street; economists recognize it; hell, even Wall Street bankers recognize it. And yet, it takes a heated six-minute-and-twenty-seven-second conversation for me to get one of the country's leading voices in Congress to recognize it? What's with that?

The point is, when there is real listening, when there is conversation, it is much harder for the funny talk to get through unchallenged.

That is what this book is about, how the new America—you—has had it with the old way of politicians getting by with just echoing the same talking points, however illogical their arguments may be, and never having to answer or explain themselves.

Let me give you another example.

▓ Ensign's Mistress

I interviewed Senator John Ensign, who cheated on his wife. Here is one of Nevada's senior statesman, who talked his friend and his friend's wife into following him from California to Nevada, where he hires them both. He makes his best friend, Doug Hampton, his top aide and his top aide's wife, Cynthia Hampton, his campaign treasurer. He then admits that Cynthia is also his lover, and basically that he had betrayed his friend Doug Hampton. You following this?

There's more. When the affair threatens to get ugly and public, he tries to shut it down by having a check written to the Hamptons for $96,000. Here's a guy who voted to impeach Bill Clinton for the Lewinsky scandal, but he's not willing to deal squarely with his own peccadillo.

Senator Ensign is confronted by Senator Tom Coburn, and according to the *New York Times*, he's ordered to end the affair or Coburn will "go to Mitch," referring to Mitch McConnell, the Republican Senate leader. Ensign agrees, and according to the *New York Times*, he writes a letter to Cynthia Hampton and sends it by overnight mail. "What I did with you was a mistake," he spells out in longhand. "I was completely self-centered and only thinking of myself. I used you for my own pleasure."

Done deal, right? No, immediately after sending the letter, he tells Cynthia Hampton to disregard it. And his relationship with her carries on for another six months. Coburn, who's an ordained minister, tells the *Times* that "John got trapped doing something really stupid." Then he added this gem about his buddy: "Judgment gets impaired by arrogance, and that's what's going on here."

So did I ask John Ensign about any of the above during our interview? No, but I did ask him about health care, and then I shifted over to what seemed most pressing, and unfortunately for him . . . difficult. His personal life is his business. What *is* my business, and yours, are allegations of public malfeasance, and a law that says Senate aides are not allowed to lobby within a year of leaving their jobs. What was Doug Hampton doing? He was lobbying. And who, according to

Hampton got him those lobbying gigs and actually set up his meetings to lobby public officials? Ensign did. Was he trying to shut Ensign up?

That's what I wanted to ask him about. Ensign was so shocked by the questioning that all he could do was half smile and tell me to look at the record, even though this was his first official interview on the subject, and as senior writer Gary Daughters pointed out to me, there really was no record. "It's your job to establish the record," Daughters explained. "And he's hoping you don't push him!" I did push him.

The confrontation went viral overnight.

What was the fuss about? I did my homework and asked some very direct questions of the senator, which last time I checked is what I'm paid to do, right? I didn't ask tough questions about him cheating on his wife. I couldn't give a hoot about that, even if he did vote to impeach Bill Clinton for it. I asked questions about something much more impactful. Allegations that Ensign assisted and encouraged a former staffer to lobby within one year of leaving his position. Why is that a big deal? Oh, let's see, maybe because it's against the friggin' law? You bet it is. And every U.S. senator knows that law—including Senator Ensign.

What I hear from you is that you're sick of it. You tell me this is exactly the kind of straightforward questioning that you want, that you demand. I listen to you and together we make people like Ensign listen to us.

At least Ensign came on and took questions. I wish I could say the same about former senator and presidential candidate John Edwards. We called the once popular Democrat's office repeatedly to ask him about reports that he may have used campaign funds to carry on a scandalous affair with his mistress/cinematographer, but he refused to come on the show. Reports later surfaced that he'd fathered a child with Rielle Hunter, and she agreed to a spread detailing the affair in *GQ* magazine. The tabloids seemed to own the story, and we were not able to get him on the record. Believe me, it wasn't for lack of trying.

■ Obama and "My BO"

I must admit, I got the idea of listening to you, and connecting with you through social media, from somebody else. You may have heard of him. His name is Barack Obama. I don't know if he's going to turn out to be a good, bad, or mediocre president—that's for historians to decide.

But of this, I'm convinced, historians will agree on: Obama did set a new standard for political campaigning, and devised a whole new model for accomplishing it. He used social media to raise money, to interact with people, to hear what they were talking about, to respond to them and to get them out to vote. And while he was a Democratic contender, what he did was so new, so extraordinary, and so absolutely unheard of that it even took the Democratic Party by surprise.

I started picking up on what he was doing as I watched him win primaries and caucuses in a way that seemed driven by social media.

I found it extraordinary and began looking into it to possibly do a story about it.

Of course, many in my profession were not convinced and seemed to be asking: "Why are you making it sound like *only* Barack Obama is using social media?"

I said, "No, it's not that he's the only one using it, but he does seem to have come as close as anybody ever has to successfully integrating it in the political process."

It's important to note that before Obama, in the 2004 campaign, presidential candidate Howard Dean was heralded as the first national candidate to successfully use the Internet to campaign. He collected a massive database of seemingly eager and willing progressives.

Without social media, though, was he able to seal the deal? Seemingly not.

The technology that existed at the time did not allow his grassroots organizers to work independently of the campaign by organizing themselves as Obama's campaign was able to do, according to experts who study the development of social media trends. It's a screaming shame. So sorry, couldn't help myself. (Dean's campaign came to a bizarre end in Iowa when he began yelling and screaming like a madman on national television about not giving up and "continuing on." It ended with a guttural, primeval screech, which turned the presidential front-runner, scholar, and physician, fairly or unfairly, into every late-night comedian's punching bag.)

Here's the deal on the general analysis of the difference between Dean and Obama—and this is important because it's the model I used to marry social and mainstream media: Candidate Dean used the Internet to collect money (and he likely would have done more if social media had been more prominent at the time), but Obama used it to collect people.

With Twitter, MySpace, and Facebook, candidate Obama used the Internet to collect people, though not everyone who tweeted me thought it was so genius . . .

(Obama use of social media) overhyped.

Obamas use of social media was genius.

▓ Social Media as Campaign Tool

I tried explaining to many of my colleagues and friends how it seemed Obama's application of the Internet was different because he tied it to social media to create a community following.

Many of them, however, would have none of it. Many of them argued that John McCain uses social media "and even has a Twitter page too."

"Yes, yes, he does," I answered. "You're right. He has a Twitter page. But it's not the same as Obama's Twitter page." I pointed out that McCain's Twitter page had been created by staff members in response to Obama's social media campaign.

I told them that Obama had more than one million people following him on Twitter, while McCain was on the record saying that when it comes to using a computer, he is "an illiterate who has to rely on his wife for all the assistance he can get." That hardly makes McCain a lesser candidate, but it did make him less capable of integrating social media.

I tried making the point that Obama seemed more tech-savvy, carries a BlackBerry and a laptop everywhere he goes, and McCain, according to his own interviews, didn't use a laptop and needed an aide to handle and work his BlackBerry for him. I suggested it was unfair to bring McCain into the argument, that it was actually unfair to McCain. Technologically speaking, he wasn't in Obama's league. It was like me trying to compare my skills to my sixteen-year-old son Robby's on Guitar Hero. Forget about it!

It may be understood now. But back during the 2008 campaign, not everyone was catching the nuance of the political power of social media.

By the way, Obama's staffers may have begun the trend. But it's not exclusive to him. One of the largest grassroots movements since the sixties developed with two words: "tea parties." It was organized and executed mainly on the Internet with, you guessed it, social media. Their collectivism and use of new technology to organize was brilliant and will likely set the standard for many grassroots efforts to come.

You'll notice that social media is not the domain of the right or the left. Maybe that's what makes it work. And it makes me and my colleagues who incorporate it at CNN more balanced. Although, as I read from your tweets, we can't convince everybody.

> (CNN) leans liberal. FOX leans conservative. If I wanted it any other way, I'd watch C-Span.

> It seems that CNN can be too liberal, & that's not a good thing. Being conservative means God-intended values are being kept.

> CNN is the most balanced of all the news networks.

League of First-Time Voters

My political assignment at CNN during the 2008 campaign was to travel the country in search of first-time voters. It became a weekly CNN staple called, appropriately enough, "The League of First Time Voters."

This is where I really got to understand the power of Obama's social media reach.

Why? Because it was so easy for us to fill a room with young voters who were supporters of candidate Obama. But it was tough as hell to fill a room with first-time voters who were supporters of John McCain.

I remember watching my field producers, Michael Heard and Jason Morris, looking absolutely exasperated after making hours' and hours' worth of calls looking for a panel of young McCain supporters. I swear to God, it was like finding teenagers hanging out at a bingo hall. Just ain't going to happen.

This is how Morris describes the experience . . .

It was difficult to find enough motivated young republicans to help us balance out our panels. It took many hours of research, phone calls, e-mails, facebook messages, etc. And within most of these groups it was still very difficult to find young, motivated, conservative voices. What wound up happening was we would have a plethora of great options on the democratic side, but be stuck using any republican supporters who were willing to talk to us on camera (not sure if you want to put that in print or not, but that's the truth). In retrospect, and after many hours on the phone—we made it work!

That doesn't mean we didn't work hard to find supporters on both sides regardless of their age. Here's a sampling of the groups we talked to: Southerners from traditionally conservative backgrounds; Mennonites in Goshen, Indiana; immigration voters in Phoenix; African-American students in Atlanta; Muslim Americans in Detroit; Jewish students in Chicago; environmentalists; evangelicals; Cuban Americans; Indian Americans; and nurses.

If John McCain knew how hard we worked to find his young supporters, he probably would have tried to hire us. I'll tell you this, though, in the interest of fairness, we always found a way to make it work. And boy, did we ever rack up SkyMiles.

While we were scouring the country in search of young McCain supporters, Barack Obama was having supporters come to him, hundreds of thousands of them. And they were doing it on the Internet. He talked to somebody in Austin, Texas, who branched out and created an online community of people *he* talked to—and those people branched out and created more communities, and so on and so on, eventually creating this emergent network of Barack Obama supporters who were also volunteers. And the beauty of it was most of them didn't need to be visited or sent money or organized from campaign headquarters; they did most of it on their own.

Now I should mention, Sarah Palin's addition to the GOP ticket did in fact encourage many younger and first-time voters to side with the McCain camp, but by then there was too much catching up to do.

Fact is, Obama won two of every three voters under the age of thirty, according to the exit polls. This was part of Obama's social media revolution. Many now argue it set the stage, and that never again will a candidate consider running for office without a sophisticated virtual reach that incorporates social media!

Say what you want about President Barack Obama, but what you can't say is that when it came to using the principles of community organizing toward the goal of winning the presidency, he and his campaign didn't master social media as a political tool. And what is social media if not a virtual version of community organizing?

We (social media) are like any other community.
Some hide and talk only to those who think like them
while others enjoy open communication.

I think you could use Twitter 4 that, look at what u r
doing, communication that's what its 4.

Hell, one of the first things Obama did was bring in Chris Hughes, the cofounder of Facebook, as one of his campaign strategists. Hughes developed the most advanced Web-based networking tools ever used in a political campaign. Hughes, who was appropriately described by *Rolling Stone* magazine as a teen-faced, blue-eyed wunderkind, invented MyBarackObama.com, or MyBo, and yes, during the campaign of 2008, it became the rage.

Talk about branding. Many who felt like they had been politically disenfranchised by the old political model had their own community to join. And join they did. MyBo allowed energized citizens to turn themselves into activists with nothing but a laptop or a mobile phone. It was an attractive, fun Web site that allowed Obama supporters to create groups, plan events, raise funds, download tools, and connect with one another. And the most ingenious part of it was they could do it on their own, without a traditional field staffer. The young, especially, flocked to it. Yeah, but would it really make a difference at the polls? At the time, nobody really knew, and many doubted it.

Iowa was its first test. Dr. Michael Eric Dyson is a scholar and respected intellectual, a guy with a mesmerizing delivery, who said this to me back in 2007, when I asked him about Obama's chances: "We know when white people get in that booth and pull that curtain, they will not vote for a black man no matter what they're telling pollsters."

Realistically, few Americans, even among those who voted for him, thought Obama could actually win before the Iowa caucus. But it seemed to Dyson that the biggest segment of Obama skeptics were blacks. They just didn't believe white people would vote for a black guy, therefore eliminating Obama from consideration as a viable candidate. In short, many blacks would not vote for Obama, because they didn't think enough whites would vote for him. It's that simple.

But Iowa changed the game. It sent a message to blacks, most of whom were, according to polls, supporting Hillary Rodham Clinton, that it was okay to get behind Obama. Hell, if Iowans, who are a whopping 96 percent white, can vote for Obama, then you bet his support among blacks would catch fire, and catch fire it did.

Not everyone believed Iowa was a game changer. Reverend Jesse Jackson took my call and appeared with me the night after Obama's big Iowa win. He was the perfect get. While many Americans, thanks to FOX News and talk radio, have unfairly come to regard him exclusively as a black activist, he was more than Obama's equal at the time. Jackson, the guy used by the right wing to rile up or scare white people, won an impressive eleven states during the 1988 Democratic primaries and had come in third in 1984 behind Walter Mondale and Gary Hart. If anybody could offer perspective and analysis on what it was like for a black candidate to win a big primary, you'd think it would be Reverend Jackson.

So here I was on TV, analyzing Obama's unique win and his distinctive community-based approach with members of Obama's Harlem team of organizers. They were psyched and they got it. Reverend Jackson, as Borat would say, "not so much."

Here was Jackson, the guy who walked side by side with Dr. Martin Luther King, yet the generational divide between him and the young black computer-savvy voters supporting Obama might as well have been a hundred miles. They were that far apart. Jackson was tempering their enthusiasm. The man who was there on the balcony in Memphis when King was assassinated wasn't quite ready to pass the mantle, and he didn't.

The newscast's guests seemed to suggest that Obama was on fire, but the day after the Jackson interview, I received an e-mail from a colleague suggesting my analysis was "naïve," that Obama's Iowa win was akin to "a fluke" and that the suggestion that Obama could be a legitimate front-runner was incorrect because there was still a long way to go. That was true, but I was hearing from many of you that Iowa had unleashed the black vote. Regardless, the criticism stung. I swallowed hard and bit my lip, but Obama proceeded to win twelve caucuses in a row between February and March. The Obama social media strategy seemed invincible. My gut was right. Why? Because caucuses like the ones in Iowa and Texas, and all those in between, were about community organizing. It was a parallel model for social media organizing. You got it, and I got it. Americans could organize themselves and then go out and cast communal votes, as opposed to voting at the ballot box.

After the election everybody was talking about the Republicans and how they could recuperate and what this meant and blah, blah, blah. You suggested it seemed like conventional idiocy. The reality was that even the Democrats were sitting there going, "Are we the

Democratic Party? Or are we the Obama Party now?" There was this populist thing that happened and the Democrats got swept up in a flood toward the top. And when it was over, they were left looking around nervously, wondering, "What happens now?"

It was transformational. Of course, transformations don't last forever.

Obama found it more difficult to mobilize his social media base in his first year in office toward other goals, like passing legislation. But what he achieved during the campaign through social media was a spark that sent many scurrying to know more about social media as a legitimate technique that could be used in politics and, as I discovered, in news.

What the Hell Does Twitter Have to Do with Real News?

In August 2008, the producer Chris Hall, a guy much hipper and more Internet-savvy than me, introduced me to social media, through My-Space and Facebook. He was convinced we should somehow incorporate it into our newscasts.

But every time I went to Facebook and MySpace, I found it to be very long-winded and more about personal stories that really didn't fit the broadcast news model. They weren't really talking that much about the news. And when they were, the conversations were too long to edit into good TV.

That summer, though, at the Hispanic Journalists Convention in Chicago, where I was asked to speak, Jon Klein, the president of CNN USA, asked me to meet him for breakfast. Klein said to me, "Hey, have you heard about this thing called Twitter?"

"No," I said. "What is it?"

"Twitter is really different," he said. "It's a part of social media called micro-blogging, where people talk to each other about what they're doing, but they do it in short sentences. You ought to look into it."

Well, I thought, "That's cool, the president of the company likes this Twitter thing, or else he wouldn't have brought it to my attention."

The following weekend, I went back to Chris Hall and said, "Tell me everything you know about Twitter."

He said, "It's the newest thing out there. Nobody really knows what to do with it, but the few people who use it are really going crazy with it."

I asked, "Well, what do I do?"

And he said, "Why don't I create a Twitter account for you and ask the people who are out there already on Twitter to join you?" Then he asked, "Doesn't Klein have to sign off on this?"

"Trust me," I said. "He already has. Why do you think I'm asking you about it?"

That night, we put a show on the air with an open laptop on the set in front of me. It was opened to my Twitter account and I invited viewers to join me at twitter.com/ricksanchezcnn.

Lo and behold, people started shooting me tweets in the middle of the newscast, reacting, sharing! First fifty followers, then a hundred, then a couple thousand, and before the week's end I had more than five thousand people engaged and corresponding with me while I was on the air.

The Hurricane Tweets

Then Hurricane Gustav hit and it broke wide open.

The *Miami Herald* said: "Rick Sanchez, Success with Twitter and TV."

This is September 2, 2008. The *Herald*'s TV reviewer continued: "Somebody had to take the big step at CNN and actually do it. Not only did Rick Sanchez take the first step, but he's also making it successful. He's fusing Twitter into CNN news and no one has ever done this before."

CNN's public relations gurus were downright giddy that we were getting this kind of press. Twitter, huh, who knew?

Here's what got us the *Miami Herald* accolade. Hurricane Gustav was about to hit the Florida panhandle, New Orleans, and parts of Alabama. And because authorities were still in a post-Katrina mindset, they called for a massive evacuation.

On the air, I reported the evacuation and then asked evacuees to reach out to me on Twitter. "Use your laptop, your BlackBerry, your phone, whatever," I urged. "Just let me know what's going on out there."

Suddenly, I receive several tweets from motorists stuck for miles and miles in an accident on Interstate 65 in Alabama. They tell me it's a parking lot. People are starting to panic that they'll be trapped there, run out of gas, or worse, that the hurricane will come up behind them.

Right there on camera, I turn to the crew manning the National Desk in the CNN headquarters behind me and scream out: "I'm getting tweets telling me there's a huge accident and that people should not take Interstate 65, or they could be trapped and backed up there for hours and they're worried they'll be trapped by the hurricane."

"What's a tweet?" one smart-ass producer queried. But moments later, they had it nailed down. Alabama Highway Patrol confirmed the report. It was true. And by working with police and our CNN affiliate TV stations, and by getting the word out to hundreds of thousands of people listening to CNN being simulcast on the radio, evacuees were able to receive information and respond to alternate routes being funneled by Alabama's finest.

It was the first real bona fide case where social media and old media were successfully merged to cover, if not break and resolve, a legitimate story. Twitter, this newfangled way to talk to each other in minibursts of 140 characters at a time, had just been used to provide crucial, up-to-the-minute information that may have possibly saved some lives—which is ultimately what news needs to do.

The Power of Social Media

"Rick, this is getting scary," the voice on the other end of the phone screamed out. Joe Wendich was driving away from a canyon near L.A., where thousands of residents were being evacuated because of a massive wildfire that seemed uncontrollable.

Every network newscast was leading with the Southern California fires, but only Wendich could describe it from the inside where it had jumped the fire line. It was news in the making and Wendich was explaining what was happening live and only on CNN. I had tweeted that morning, asking people to reach out to me, and I started getting a bunch of people who said, "Oh my God, Rick, I'm afraid I'm going to lose my home."

Wendich was one of fifty Twitter followers from the scene who responded. He was a volunteer who was in the middle of it, helping everybody else. He was tweeting from the scene and he was describing how the flames were rising out of the canyons. I had connected with him that morning, and by three in the afternoon, he was ready to go live.

CNN viewers watched the live aerial video feeds of homes being decimated, while listening to Wendich on the phone describing how the fire was increasing in both strength and size. He was telling the story from the inside and nobody could compete with him.

This was the power of social media. Joe wasn't a reporter. He wasn't an official reading statistics. He was a real person, who I had been tweeting with since morning, who knew the story and was describing what he was experiencing firsthand. It also wasn't me talking; it was "we" talking.

■ "Don't Piss on My Leg and Tell Me It's Raining!"

As our show grew, and as people started to latch on to this different thing that we were doing, we started to hear particularly passionate feedback from our viewers about a few issues more than any others. The power of social media had already been made clear to us with our coverage of the disasters like the hurricane and the fires, but those were small-time compared to the disaster that was the financial collapse of 2008. And ever since, it's been economy, economy, economy.

Throughout this book, you'll recognize the different aspects of the "conventional idiocy" that many of you say you're sick of. From you I hear your frustrations with politicians, your money, and the systems that seem unchangeable. You tell me you are angry about Wall Street, and I understand.

Too big to fail, my ass. That's what most Americans scream about when they tweet me about the line they were fed in the fall of 2008. The thought process crystallized when in the fall of the following year, those same Wall Street bankers whose butts we bailed out with our money began awarding themselves record bonuses once again. Yep, you heard it right. In less than a year, we went from being told our entire banking system as we knew it was on the brink of collapse to Wall Streeters earning record compensation packages, while the rest of the country's business was still in the dumps. Nice!

It's not that we didn't want our banks to succeed, we did. It's just that on its face it seems reprehensible that the same people who created the problem became the first to cash out—with *our* money. How can you look at that and not say it stinks? It's as easy as one, two, and three. Here's how leading economists explain it:

One: To create unfair advantages for themselves, Wall Streeters got our politicians, both Dems and Republicans, to change the laws and eliminated many regulatory processes, making it harder for us to keep the banks in check.

Two: To game the system, bankers, investors, and accountants created something called credit default swaps, which are legal but we now know allowed credit ratings to be given to bundled toxic mortgages that we also now know didn't deserve to be treated as if they were "safe."

Three: Too many regulators didn't do their jobs. And many financial experts told me it was because some regulators allowed themselves to be wooed by the promise of jobs on Wall Street. This wasn't true of all regulators, but for some it was like the fox guarding the henhouse.

Voilà! There you have it, the simple formula for an economic meltdown. And most of you have plenty to say about it, and plenty to blame:

> dems will never get my vote if they don't pass it
> (financial reform).

Now, for those of you who like to play the blame game, there's plenty to go around. And you blame them all.

Republicans? Yes!

Democrats? Absolutely!

President Clinton? No question!

President Bush/Cheney? (Can you say one name without the other?) Affirmative!

Now, I could go into a lengthy explanation with lots of numbers and details and names like TARP, 700 billion, Citigroup, Wells

Fargo, Summers, Paulson, Geithner, and so on. Trust me, I will later in this book. But for now, let's just look at it for what it is with an expression you hear plenty down here in the South—I live in Atlanta—especially from my golf buddy Mark Darrow. Darrow's favorite refrain: "Don't piss on our legs and then try to tell us it's raining!"

Follow the Money

You've told me to ask questions and "follow the money." Well, here they are: Which politicians—from either party—vote most consistently to benefit Wall Street? The politicians who get the most money from Wall Street, that's who, according to OpenSecrets.org.

Which politicians voted most consistently for the health insurance industry and health-care companies who didn't want the public option to pass? Though most seem to get money from just about everybody, there did seem to be a correlation between those who voted against the public option and those who got the most campaign financing money.

I could go on and on. Lawyers, unions, drug makers. The list is only limited by our political system's voracity for campaign funds, which is, as you probably know by now, bottomless!

What I have discovered from asking these questions is as much a result of your work as it is mine, because you have given me the push, the impetus to look into what has made you angry:

> I think (journalism) much better with Social Media.
> Now that you (rick) have started it you can't go back.

> I like how you show tweets, etc. from people in-
> volved in the stories you report on. Not so much
> public opinion. That gets old.

Old News Versus "You" News

Journalists are funny. Many journalists who I've met over the thirty years I've spent working in the business tend to think that we have proprietary ownership over the news. Like it's ours. We own it and we're going to share it with people because we're the experts.

But I believe it's important for us to collect as many of your collective thoughts as we can.

You're not professional news gatherers. But you are eyewitnesses to history, experts in a thousand fields, and—most important—you are the foremost experts in the world about what's important to you.

And that's what this book is about, the issues that you tell me are the most important to *you*.

BlackBerrys and Kindles

Remember those images of the Berlin Wall coming down? People swinging sledgehammers to break away the concrete? It came apart a chunk at a time. Then the first people squeezed through an opening and you could see the daylight. That's what's happening now with the news. The people in the social media networks are smashing the walls of traditional journalism.

But among old-guard journalists, there is this quiet conspiracy of resistance. They just don't get it. It's not part of their generation. It's not something that they're familiar with. And it's certainly not something that they learned coming up as reporters.

It's not a seamless transition, but it's the way the world is changing. It's the way people are talking to one another today, and it's the way people are going to be talking in the future. People will be using their cell phones, their iPhones, their BlackBerrys, their laptops, and their Kindles while they're watching the news or reading the newspapers. They will check you. They will talk to others. They will share your information with other people.

The whole thing is a circle now. It's not a line that starts at A and ends at B. It's now a complete circle that is constantly going around and never ends. It truly is a national conversation.

And it was from that conversation that this book was born. With *Conventional Idiocy*, I have taken everything I've learned from the conversation we have on the show, everything I've absorbed from listening to you.

■ The Cyber-Porch

It really is a new world. It's the future based on something we've somehow lost with each generation for over a hundred years or more. What did they have back then that we are missing now? Community. That's right, our parents, our grandparents, and our great-grandparents all kept in touch with friends and family, with each other. It's how they constructed ideas. It's how they formed their values. It's how they associated with one another.

So what happened to us? With TV and radio, Americans did get something that involved audience response, but it's not the same as social media, because social media allows you to engage with us and each other.

All this time we thought we were getting more connected than ever before in history, and we were actually fooling ourselves, or being fooled. We had actually never been so unconnected. We really were tuning each other out and relying on one-way communication. We chose to listen to a speech rather than be a part of a conversation. And in the process, we lost the power of "us."

Many of you are probably thinking, "Wasn't it the Internet that empowered us?" The answer is yes and no. Think of it this way. I describe social media as dot-com-plus, because we thought the dot-com era was a tectonic change, a new and revolutionary way to receive information. And we were right. But it only got us halfway there.

Like all previous forms of mass communication going back to Gutenberg's printing press, it delivered, but we weren't able to communicate among ourselves.

Until social media came along, the only thing that we had to go with was mass media. And mass media in any form, whether it's newspapers or television or radio, basically made us consumers of a linear message. It is one-way communication. In other words, we will sit and will listen to the radio. We will sit on the couch and watch TV. We will sit and read this newspaper, but how do we talk to each other?

It's all one-way. It's coming at you, not from you!

Mass media converted us into a nation of information consumers, which left little room for dialogue.

Again, yes, even the Internet was at fault—it opened thousands of doors, but it was still just one way in. We visited CNN.com to read stuff, much the same as we watch it on CNN. Or we visited the *New York Times* site and read the *New York Times*. Well, that's the same as reading the paper. Or we'd visit the Home Depot Web site to get information about or place an order for a lightbulb or to Joe's Pizza to order a pie.

Yes, there were chat rooms and the like, but nothing so radically transformed the flow of information as social media. For the first time in our history, we are able to link together in vast, global networks and communicate simultaneously. We engage, as opposed to just consume. It's not one-way. It's all-way. It's a community.

Where it's taking us remains to be seen. It really is still brand-new. We're in the process of changing because the technology is changing. Just as the printing press changed the way we exchanged information, and broadcast television accelerated the pace of that exchange to the speed of light, this new simultaneous and instantaneous interaction that allows you to communicate with others like you via social media may be permanently altering how we communicate in ways we may not even be able to imagine.

That's got a lot of people, from politicians and teachers to religious leaders and mass media moguls, more than a bit nervous. You'll see it over and over again in this book. People who benefit from the old ways and the old politics don't want to acknowledge this new America. Because it's true: Information is power. And if every one of us can speak to and hear from one another, the people who have traditionally controlled the flow of information suddenly have a whole lot of competition.

Hurricane Katrina, If Only

Think about this. Hurricane Katrina was a disaster. However, it would have been less likely to have wound up as such a communication disaster if it happened today. New Orleans residents could have used social media to communicate their story early and often, just as Iranians used Twitter to tell the world of their plight by sending images called twitpics around the globe.

Here's why I know Katrina could and should have been different. In 2005, as fate would have it, on Monday, August 29, I was on the set anchoring the news in the wee hours of the morning when the levees (and all hell) broke loose in New Orleans. I broke the news during an interview with the president of Tulane University that New Orleans was flooding because the levees were breached.

CNN's comprehensive coverage of the disaster won a Peabody for breaking news. The next day there was work to do. I flew to the disaster zone and hit the ground running.

Years earlier, I had learned the power of storytelling following a natural disaster while covering Hurricane Andrew in South Florida. Our coverage back then, which combined reporting the personal stories of loss and organizing an on-air relief effort on WSVN-TV, won me recognition from the Florida Association of Broadcasters and a "1000 points of light recognition award" from President George H. W. Bush. All I did was use mass media, through my broadcast signal, to organize a desperate community and connect victims with people who wanted to help them. The experience would serve me well.

Back now to Katrina. Several days into the flooding, I began filing stories from some of the outlying areas. Producer Michael Heard and I waded into waters where bloated bodies floated by. We boarded rickety skiffs while covering rescues, and heard the constant screams of women and children stuck in attics begging to be saved. Some were rescued, some weren't. The boats were too few, and the screams too frequent. The screams still keep me up at night.

The government let the people of New Orleans down by taking too long and doing too little in those early days. And some in the media misinterpreted the desperate cries for help for something else. We should have been listening, connecting, and helping to organize a community in need. Instead, too many in the media focused on looting and desperation depicted as violence in the New Orleans Superdome. If only we'd had the vehicle to know just how desperate the people of New Orleans really were. We misinterpreted their desparation.

Today, it might have been different. With social media and nothing more than a cell phone, the people we called looters could have talked back. They could have told their stories, described their needs, and helped us understand their plight.

The Revolution Is Here

Some say the social media revolution will change the way we interact. I say they're looking in the wrong direction. The change is in the rearview mirror. It already *has*.

When we engage in those communities of friends and followers, whether it's through Twitter or MySpace or Facebook or whatever, we find a receptive, eager, and really smart group of people. And it does what neither newspapers, nor the old radio model, nor the old TV news model, nor even the Internet by itself was ever able to achieve. We no longer will talk *to* viewers, we'll talk *with* viewers. And they will talk back.

Many of my colleagues and managers at CNN were obviously a bit suspicious at the outset of my using social media. But we also became among the first in the industry to embrace it, because while some believe that watching television news is becoming passé, being part of television news is not.

You're now connected and will likely not allow us, or your government leaders, to pull one over on you. You're hungry for real information and want insight about the things you genuinely do care about.

The following chapters are intended to provide just that. You ask me to ask the tough questions, to challenge the people who I interview—so that's what I've tried to do here. You tell me you're sick of the old thinking and the old politics.

Things may be changing. Today it seems like every politician from John McCain to your local mayor has a Twitter account. It seems anybody who wants to get elected is going to have to connect on social media, and will have to be transparent about it. But they'll have to be careful, because that virtual constituency is a lot tougher to fool. You're informed, you're engaged, and you're demanding answers and accountability.

You are the new America and you won't settle for the old politics of business as usual.

CHAPTER 1

You're Sick of
Blind Partisanship

When the philosopher Friedrich Nietzsche penned "Many are stubborn in pursuit of the path he's chosen, few in pursuit of the goal," you'd think he was studying American politics in 2010! Doesn't that nail it? These folks will argue from their ideological base, regardless of truth, regardless of facts, regardless of common sense, and maybe most important of all, regardless of what's good for the country.

You tell me you're sick of the blind partisanship. You tell me about America's elected officials and how their proxies don't actually communicate—they just keep yelling at each other. They keep pointing fingers. They use simpleton slogans and meaningless labels. They use race, patriotism, and religion, whatever it takes to win the moment, but not a lasting change.

Remember George W. Bush's bullhorn moment. You know the one I'm talking about. It's where the president, after looking confused after being told about 9/11 while reading *My Pet Goat* to a bunch of Florida schoolkids, found his footing a full three days later surrounded by rescue workers amid the debris of the Twin Towers.

"The world hears you," Bush screamed out with his arm around a firefighter. "And the people who knocked these buildings down will hear all of us soon." It was great TV news fodder, a moment that may have sparked the zeal within the president to act with more bravado going forward. After all, up until that moment, the CNN polls showed—and many in the media had concluded—that the forty-third president of the United States was not exactly lighting it up with the American people.

About that same time, as President Bush was exercising his first taste of certitude, an ideology that would drive him for five years into his administration, a future president was sitting in his law office writing a statement about the 9/11 attack. Barack Obama, the unknown Illinois state senator, was writing about the need to dismantle the "organizations of destruction," and described the attackers as having "a fundamental absence of empathy." But he also wrote about the need for "understanding the sources of such madness," understanding these "embittered children."

Some say Obama's more cerebral approach lacks passion. But in fairness to President Bush, one other important note should be made for comparative purposes: It's easy to be cool-headed when you're not in the battle; Obama was not.

(Obama's) lack of certitude & early vocal muscle makes things messy, confusing & much longer, but what matters is resolve.

A Bush approach probably would've had health-care reform passed by now.

It's not clear how historians will treat President Bush. But there is no denying what even Bush himself has pointed out, that his fervor to respond aggressively and sound tough did at times backfire. Certitude is great in the moment, but not so great in the long run.

Certitude was President Bush calling the war "a crusade." Oops! Fair or unfair, that word reverberated around the Arab and Muslim world like a megaton bomb.

Certitude was also a Dick Cheney trait, maybe best displayed when he said to his colleague Senator Patrick Leahy on the Senate floor, "Go fuck yourself." Leahy was questioning him about the military contractor Halliburton, of which Cheney was the former CEO.

Moments are just that, moments. They're great for cable news, but they provide little by way of understanding. More often than not, they're just an opportunity for a politician to play his usual hand. Democrats habitually answer my questions by sticking to their partisan talking points. And Republicans do the same. Sometimes I wonder why I invited them in the first place; I might as well have asked and answered the questions myself. Hell, I usually know what they're going to say. And they rarely disappoint.

What our elected officials don't understand is that some of you want the conversation to move beyond the usual politics. You—the new, connected America—want it that way. Some of you make the argument that the old systems are splintering. We witnessed it in District 23 in upstate New York, and with Joe Lieberman breaking away from the Democratic Party, and Arlen Specter breaking away from the GOP. What it seems to illustrate is that conventional wisdom is being challenged. Many of you are calling for representation based on ideas, not on parties.

Many of you tweet me daily, pushing me to cover less of the process and more of the ideas. You ask all of us in my profession to call things as they are, and I've tried to take you up on it.

"Birther" Partisanship

Too often ideological bullshit can dominate the discussion unchallenged. My job is to be annoyed enough to challenge those I interview. One of the best examples of ideological hackery occurred shortly after the inauguration of Barack Obama, with what came to be known as the "birther" movement. If you really look into the facts, it makes you just want to scream. It was ridiculous—and outrageous. And I felt compelled to go on television and set the record straight.

I was embarrassed that I had to, and I said so.

"There is something strange about even having to do this story," I said during the segment that ran on July 21, 2009. "So, for those of you who get this, please, we apologize. But it has gotten to the point where there are so many people in this country who believe this that it needs to be addressed."

I showed a video clip that made me feel that I just had to do something to debunk this myth. It showed a woman at what was supposed to be a town hall meeting about the then proposed health-care-reform legislation. It was meant to give folks a chance to ask Republican representative Mike Castle of Delaware questions about the proposals then making their way through both chambers of Congress.

But in the middle of it all, an older woman stands up and hits him with this completely off-topic and, I might add, off-base question.

"I want to go back to January twentieth, and I want to know why you people are ignoring his birth certificate," she said. "He is not an American citizen. He is a citizen of Kenya."

And people in the audience started cheering and applauding.

Incredible!

Castle—a Republican, no less—seemed taken aback.

"If you're referring to the president there," he said, "he is a citizen of the United States."

He tried to get back to the reason they were supposed to all be there, to talk about health care, but she didn't want to. Instead, she invited the people in the audience to stand and recite the Pledge of Allegiance—and they did! As if to say, "We are behind you one hundred percent. We want America back from this illegitimate president."

I began the segment by holding up an official copy of Barack Obama's birth certificate, verified by FactCheck.org. The nonpartisan organization met with officials in Honolulu. They examined all available documents and they unequivocally found that the president was born in Hawaii.

I held up the "certificate of birth," as they call it in Hawaii, and had a cameraman zoom in so the folks at home could see it, and I showed people: "Child's name, Barack Hussein Obama II. . . . You see he was born at seven twenty-four p.m. There, it says the island of birth, Oahu. There it says when he was born, August 1961. His parents . . ." And so on.

I presented aloud all the pertinent facts and pointed to the data on the birth certificate so the viewers could follow along.

Then I said why I was doing it: "To a large and vocal group of Americans, this paper that I just showed you might as well be bathroom tissue. Factual, maybe. Enough to stop the speculation? Absolutely not.

"This completely unfounded story—let me repeat—this completely unfounded story continued to get so much play in certain media that it led to a congressman's town hall meeting actually getting hijacked."

I invited a representative from FactCheck.org who confirmed the information on air. But here's the clincher: a clipping from a Hawaii newspaper announcing Barack Obama's birth with his parents' names and address on it was also part of the record. The *Honolulu Advertiser* announcement of Barack Hussein Obama's birth was published August 13, 1961, on page B-6. It sealed the deal. This wasn't a debate. No more than there should be a debate on whether I'm using ten fingers as I type this book. It's a fact! Yet, I had watched as cable news shows covered this story as if it contained two sides. There was no yin and yang here, just a yawn for any self-respecting American interested in truth over political hackery.

Immediately, my segment went viral; the subject was appropriately dubbed by bloggers as "the issue that won't go away!"

I continued. "If somebody out there is saying that Barack Obama wasn't born in Hawaii, then his grandparents would have had to have faked this, knowing that someday he was going to be president and that they would have to put this in there, so in the future he could come back and say, look, he was born in Hawaii, but he wasn't really born in Hawaii."

Sounds crazy, doesn't it? You know what else is crazy? The fact that I had to even report on it. It seemed a perfect case of "the facts don't matter." The people who believed this nonsense wanted to believe it at all costs.

That's what being blind means. That's what many of you tell me you don't want.

Partisan Prayers

It was only a matter of time before some of the folks pushing the falsehood that President Obama is not a native-born American would want your money, and here it is—voilà!

A guy named Bill Keller of something called LivePrayer.com and his deliciously named sidekick, Gary Kreep, found a way to turn their anti-Obamaness into a full-blown cash machine. Honestly, I can't make this stuff up. Here was the pitch:

You would send them $30 and they would make sure that questions about President Obama, by golly, get rewarded.

You would receive a specially created "Got a Birth Certificate?" bumper sticker. Also, you can help a group called the United States Justice Foundation in their efforts to force President Obama to produce his birth certificate.

By making a gift of $30, you would enable them to send a fax on your behalf to all fifty state attorneys general and to U.S. Attorney

General Eric Holder demanding that they force President Obama to supply his official State of Hawaii birth certificate.

Go to your phone and call this number. Don't sit back and do nothing. Act now. Tell President Obama to prove where he was born.

Imagine, all that for thirty bucks. What a deal.

Wait! We did a little digging and guess what we found out about Mr. Keller, this guy who wants your money?

For starters, he was $80,000 in debt when he began his "birth certificate" venture. But it gets better. Bill Keller was convicted in 1989 for insider trading and spent two and a half years in prison.

So a guy charged with fraud is asking your grandma to send him money, and where do you think we found that information about Mr. Keller? On his own Web site. He cops to it. Getting you to send his Web site money by getting people irrationally riled up about the president of the United States. What a country! I tried to get Mr. Keller to come on the show, but he wouldn't.

> I think the ignorant ones that don't get news from all
> sides get scared easily by the ones that want to
> strike fear in them.

> Americans r easily swayed by politicians and misin-
> formation, because they know the majority of ameri-
> cans don't read.

The Dem Who Wouldn't Listen

Partisanship happens on both sides of the blue/red, conservative/liberal divide. There are people on the right who want to push their opinions on others, and people on the left who do the exact same thing. Then there's what you say makes you angriest—not being heard.

Sheila Jackson-Lee is an outspoken Democratic congresswoman from Texas who came to the forefront of the health-care debate when it was caught on tape that she was unwilling to hear the concerns of her constituents at a town hall meeting. She was so unabashed about ignoring citizens who came to hear her speak at the meeting that she actually got on the phone and started talking to one of her staff members in Washington while ignoring a question she was being asked by someone in the audience. The incident was brought to my attention by hundreds of you on social media who reached out to me with links to the recorded video clip.

She may not have seen how she was coming across, but from the angle the video was shot I could hear people in the audience asking questions, being ignored, and commenting to each other: "Can you believe this, she's not even listening, she's not even listening!"

It was painfully obvious after looking at the videotape that they were right. So I asked Congresswoman Jackson-Lee to come on.

Talk about a moment that went viral: When I challenged her and told her, "Look, you are disrespecting people, simply because you judge them. You decided that those people there weren't worth your time because they had a perspective that was different from yours."

I watched the clip from the town hall meeting. I saw citizens who only wanted their questions asked. Were they challenging her? Yeah, so what? They weren't saying that the public option that she supported was a Nazi idea. They were creating cogent arguments and asking her very good questions.

And while some were asking those questions, she didn't even give them the courtesy of listening. She wouldn't hear them out. She ignored them while talking on the phone. It seemed to me disgraceful and it needed to be said.

I think she was expecting—I don't know why—that I would allow her to not answer my question and move on. But I had no intention of moving on. I'm paid to ask questions and I'm also paid to re-ask them if I don't get an answer. Your tweets brought the story to my attention, and your tweets suggested she should explain or apologize. So I asked.

But instead of explaining or apologizing, she stuck to her talking points. It seemed like blind partisanship.

I talked to the congresswoman for a full six minutes on the air, and she didn't change her position from the first second to the last. She would not say, "I was wrong to do that. I apologize." Nor did she regret not hearing the questions that were being asked.

She seemed so transfixed on what she wanted to say that she came across as stubbornly partisan to the hundreds of thousands of people watching the interview.

School's Out

You brought Sheila Jackson-Lee to my attention and you also told me about State Senator Russell from Oklahoma.

It was a totally different issue, but that didn't really matter. Certainly not to him. He was toeing the party line.

Barack Obama was going to give a speech to schoolchildren all across America, and there was a lot of opposition.

From the Republican Party chairman of Florida, Jim Greer: "As the father of four children, I am absolutely appalled that taxpayer dollars are being used to spread President Obama's socialist ideology."

"No comrade left behind" was the headline on an article by Alicia M. Cohn of HumanEvents.com. She wrote: "What Obama says during the speech itself matters less than the fact that—in earlier speeches as well as this one—the Obama administration is targeting school students to listen and learn political lessons."

Six days before the president's speech, before any of its themes were known, the conservative writer Michelle Malkin wrote, "Obama classroom campaign. No junior lobbyist left behind."

It was the typical heated political rhetoric that we're all accustomed to from both sides. But Steve Russell, the Republican senator from Oklahoma, seemed to outdo everybody when he compared the president to "North Korea and Saddam Hussein." When you heard that, you tweeted me and asked: "For wanting to speak to schoolchildren?"

He was concerned about the White House working directly with the Department of Education to form lesson plans related to the speech. And that was a valid concern, but comparing him to Saddam Hussein seemed an overreach and highly partisan.

After a lengthy discussion on the merits of the argument, I cut right to the chase. "How can you convince me, Senator Russell, that what you're doing is something more than just being a hack, a partisan, who just hates this president, who hates Democrats, and that you just don't want this guy to do it?"

While the senator's argument about lesson plans suggested by the White House was a reasonable concern, he seemed mostly heated about the president's plans to address schoolchildren. The truth is, other presidents had done the same, including the last three Republican presidents, which Russell did not recognize.

Ronald Reagan did it in 1986. He talked about his efforts to improve the economy, about strengthening the armed forces, and about America's foreign policy.

George H. W. Bush did it in 1991. He encouraged kids to work hard in school. And guess what happened back then. Democrats did to George H. W. Bush what some Republicans were now doing to President Obama.

And to show that partisanship can cut both ways, here's what Congressman Dick Gephardt said about George H. W. Bush when he was set to address schoolkids: "The Department of Education should not be producing paid political advertising for the president; it should be helping us to produce smarter students." Gephardt was majority leader at the time.

In 2001, George W. Bush asked American schoolchildren to donate a dollar to help kids in Afghanistan.

When it was President Obama's turn to speak to schoolchildren, his message was generally apolitical. The president's speech was mostly about telling kids to stay in school and work hard.

I'd venture that most open-minded Americans would argue there's nothing wrong with kids hearing a president give them advice about staying in school. But I was stunned when my sixteen-year-old son came home and said, "Hey, Dad, the president is speaking tomorrow but we're not going to be allowed to hear it."

I said, "Why not?"

"Because," he said as he handed me a letter from the principal at the small Christian school he attends, "read this." It stated that students could stay after school if they wanted to listen to it.

As a Christian, I want my sons to grow up with the foundations that I've always had. I believe in Jesus Christ and I think it's important that my kids are getting an education that combines mores and values with solid academics.

However, it seemed unreasonable that students like my son would not be able to hear the president's speech in class.

"Who's the Last GOP President You Voted For?"

So when I was talking to State Senator Russell, I wanted to understand the rationale of those who opposed the president's speech.

I could sense his argument was coming from a mostly partisan perspective, no different than when I interviewed Democrat Sheila Jackson-Lee. So I pressed Russell, and ticked him off, inadvertently.

I said, "What about the possibility that you guys just can't stand this guy and you're going to do everything possible to fight him? What about that possibility?"

It was a big question, and he answered big. And the part that riled him up was the "you guys," and he said so. The point I was making is that he was coming at the argument as a partisan, just as it seemed Gephardt had done when he protested President Bush's address to students.

"Please define that for me," he said.

"Well," I said, "who did you vote for?"

"That's a matter of personal privilege as an American citizen," he shot back.

"Well, who was the last Democrat you voted for?" I asked.

"The last Democrat I voted for actually was a mayor in a local community race."

"Who was the last Democratic president you voted for?"

"I have not voted for a Democratic president," Russell answered. Then he took his shot. "Who is the last Republican president that you voted for?"

I told him I had voted for several Republican presidents.

I was being honest, what I've learned from you on social media you want—to be transparent. No BS.

Most Americans who heard me say that, I'm certain, thought in that moment, "He's more like me." Not because I voted for Republicans, but because most Americans are fair-minded. Most Americans will agree with Democrats and will agree with Republicans. And have voted for Democrats and have voted for Republicans.

But I find that too many of the people I interview, the people who are controlling the national conversation right now, are like this fellow Russell. They're locked into one side or the other—and facts be damned. If they're liberals, they think every Republican is out to destroy the environment and start wars. If they're conservatives, they think Democrats are all for a welfare state, big government, and gay rights.

So, when I shot back my response, I'll bet jaws dropped all over the country. Some were probably just surprised to hear a TV news anchor reveal information about himself. Hopefully, at least some looked at their TV sets in that instant and said, "Yeah, that's right, Sanchez. That's what we're supposed to be like in America. We're supposed to be voting on information. We're supposed to be voting for what's good for the country and not what's good for one particular party."

Then There's Obama. Oops!

It's hard to see ourselves without a mirror. When we surround ourselves with people and messages that only reflect and affirm our beliefs, we can be blinded. That can sometimes make it hard to see the line between right and wrong.

On July 16, 2009, Harvard faculty member Henry Louis Gates had an incident outside his house with a Cambridge police officer. At first it seemed like the officer had overreacted and assumed that because Gates was black, he was wrong. Here's what happened. A neighbor had called and complained about a suspicious person. The officer arrived at the address and found Professor Gates and tried to question him. Immediately, news accounts and pundits turned the story into a racial incident involving another white cop and a black suspect, this time a prominent Harvard professor who happened to be a friend and former associate of the president of the United States.

Most would argue that was reason enough for the president to stay out of it. But he didn't. President Obama took a side and it wasn't the cop's side. And he may have done so before knowing all the facts. He said: "The Cambridge police acted stupidly in arresting somebody when there was already proof that they were in their own home."

When I heard what the president said, my antennas shot up—especially because I had been a cop-beat reporter early in my career. I called my executive producer Angie Massie and asked, since I was just coming back to work Monday, "Has anybody looked at the police report?" I wanted to read the police report for myself. She said she'd look into it, and by morning—with the help of our CNN law-enforcement expert, Mike Brooks—I had the actual police report in my hand.

Funny how facts can get in the way of a good story, even the president's story. The police report detailed an officer just trying to do his job. He got a report of a suspicious person in a house and he investigated it. Professor Gates's own neighbor said he was cursing at the officer, suggesting he was out of control and out of line. The report highlighted the fact that the police officer did not know Professor Gates, did not know he was the home owner, and needed to see his ID to make sure he wasn't the suspicious person neighbors had complained about. Brooks and other law-enforcement experts I interviewed studied the report and concluded the officer had gone by the book.

My Twitter Board lit up with many of you castigating me for not understanding "the black experience" and taking the officer's side. I believe I was only reporting the facts, and the facts didn't seem to fit the too common scenario of a white police officer versus a black suspect. Even the president seemed to be saying as much when he invited both the officer and the professor to a "beer summit" at the White House to smooth things over.

As many of you tweeted, "the president took sides without knowing the facts," thereby becoming a partisan himself. Was he a victim of his own stereotypes, as many of you suggested? Some of you even tweeted that the president was, unintentionally, reinforcing what many Americans found so problematic about Reverend Wright's tirades on social justice, that they were over-the-top and stereotypical.

Look, we all make mistakes—but there's no question this incident was not President Obama's finest hour.

▪ The So-Called Bushies

It's a particular challenge not to be blinded by possible partisanship in the insular environment of a White House administration. Every president wants to be surrounded by supporters who will help carry out his mission. Presidents have to be cautious, however, that they don't surround themselves with yes-people.

Former attorney general Alberto Gonzales, his chief of staff, Kyle Sampson, and White House Counsel Harriet Miers were accused of falling into that trap under President George W. Bush. They were heavily criticized for getting caught up in a political firestorm, a move to replace some U.S. attorneys with "loyal Bushies," as Sampson referred to them in an e-mail to Miers.

The scandal that followed the dismissal of eight U.S. attorneys (one resigned after being notified he would be removed) eventually led to congressional hearings and contributed to Gonzales's resignation. Critics contended the removals were executed to either make way for attorneys more dedicated to the Republican Party or to punish ones whose actions or lack of action were considered damaging to the GOP.

As a journalist, I covered and reported on Gonzales's resignation. As a person, I felt sorry for him. Years earlier, I was invited along with other prominent Hispanics to advise him at the White House on a project to help the Bush White House better understand the problems facing young Hispanics. I found the young White House lawyer to be an extremely sensitive, smart, and caring man as we sat around a table for hours working on an initiative that was likely less pressing than the matters of state he probably spent the rest of the day on.

Now he was being accused of being complicit in a plan to boot federal prosecutors and replace them with others more loyal to the White House. White House documents released in 2009 seemed to show that Karl Rove's office had contacted Gonzales, requesting that several prosecutors be removed. Had blind partisanship apparently affected his judgment? Throughout the ordeal, Gonzales held that he "didn't recall" being asked or pressured by anyone. Someday, I hope he comes on so I can ask him.

In the end, the dismissals and the resulting resignations left a taint over a department previously considered to be independent and generally apart from influence from the White House. Because it was linked to some of the president's closest friends and highest-ranking legal officials in the administration, it left a cloud over the White House as well. And it damaged the credibility of both.

By the way, newly elected presidents have a right to remove and appoint new U.S. attorneys, and all presidents have done just that. However, they don't do it in the middle of their administrations for "highly political" reasons, as many of the now released e-mails seemed to suggest.

This is what many of you have called the effect of blind partisanship—it leads people into dark alleys. And nowhere was that more apparent than with Senator John McCain and a certain wannabe plumber from Ohio.

Joe the Plumber

Need I say more?

This guy gets in an interesting confrontation with then candidate Obama and becomes a poster child for the disaffected masses.

Good for him. He was doing what more of us journalists should do. He was challenging the candidate, with what we thought was his personal story of hardship and struggle.

It all started in the front yard of his home outside Toledo, Ohio, as Barack Obama came strolling through the neighborhood, meeting and greeting as he went. Joe Wurzelbacher stepped out of his house and, almost immediately, into the limelight. He asked the candidate about his tax plan.

"I'm looking to buy a company that makes $250, $270 to $280,000 a year," he said. "Your new tax plan is going to tax me more, isn't it?"

Within days, Obama's opponent, John McCain, made Wurzelbacher a celebrity by using him to illustrate the impact of the Democratic candidate's tax platform during the third and final presidential debate leading up to the election. It was McCain, then, who fitted Wurzelbacher with the folksy—and significantly more pronounceable—nickname we know him by today, "Joe the Plumber."

Great story. Perfect personal story for the antitax crowd.

Would have been even better, though, if it was true! Fact is, he wasn't getting ready to buy a company. What did I say about sloganeering and a lack of nuance? About getting people to buy into a moment, without thinking?

It turns out Wurzelbacher wasn't a licensed plumber at all, even though he claimed to be on his Facebook page. And he had a $1,000 personal tax lien outstanding against him.

Of course, by the time that came to light, the original "Joe the Plumber" story had already been unleashed. Unwittingly, the Republican senator from Arizona had let a genie out of the bottle, and try as he might, he couldn't stick the cork back in. Wurzelbacher's celebrity—built on a false record—was threatening to overshadow McCain's campaign.

Note to those who want to tap into the power of someone else's partisanship: Be careful what you wish for, you just might get it.

Interestingly enough, the flaws in Joe the Plumber's story—and the media scrutiny he came under—only served to make him a bigger media star.

So I invited him on my show, on election day.

The main thing I wanted to ask him about was taxes, and whether there was really any chance of him rocketing into the $250,000-plus bracket he would have to be in for any of the things he asked Obama about to affect him.

"Probably nobody in this campaign has been referred to more by his acronym, or slash name, than 'Joe the Plumber,'" I said as I introduced him. "His real name is Joe Wurzelbacher. And he's good enough to join us now to bring us up to date on what's going on with him— Joe, are you there?"

He was indeed. And he was friendly enough. I told him the truth, that when I put the word out on social media that I was going to have him on the show, a lot of people responded with questions they wanted me to ask him.

This is the question most of my viewers told me they wanted answered:

"Why would you be so upset about people who clear more than $250,000 a year having to pay taxes when you're nowhere near that category?"

"I mean, you know," he said, "they're not going to like the answer. Because it's called principles, you know? I mean that's what it comes down to to me. I don't want someone else's money. You know, let me make my money. And, you know, what if you get the opportunity to make that kind of money and all of a sudden the government is going to take it from you?"

Joe the Plumber would prove his enigmatic soul when he finally turned against the man who'd made him famous—he concluded by 2010 that McCain was just another "exploitive, elitist politician," according to *Newsweek*. Talk about biting the hand that fed you. Ouch!

◼ "You Know Who I Mean"

Those were the words of my interviewee Michael Goldfarb, then presidential candidate John McCain's deputy communications director.

He wanted Americans to believe that Barack Obama was an anti-Semite, in the vein of other African Americans who have been accused of that, like Louis Farrakhan, for example.

At the time, a controversy had flared up over Obama's connection to a guy named Rashid Khalidi. The *Los Angeles Times* reportedly got hold of a videotape of a farewell party for Khalidi, as he was leaving the University of Chicago to go work at Columbia University. According to reporter Peter Wallsten, "A special tribute came from Khalidi's friend and frequent dinner companion, the young state senator Barack Obama. Speaking to the crowd, Obama reminisced about meals prepared by Khalidi's wife, Mona, and conversations that had challenged his thinking.

"His many talks with the Khalidis, Obama said, had been 'consistent reminders to me of my own blind spots and my own biases. . . . It's for that reason that I'm hoping that, for many years to come, we continue that conversation—a conversation that is necessary, not just around Mona and Rashid's dinner table,' but around 'this entire world.'"

Seems like a typical political glad-handing message, right? Well, it turns out that before he joined the University of Chicago, Khalidi was connected with Yasser Arafat's Palestine Liberation Organization. Wallsten wrote that Khalidi frequently "spoke to reporters on behalf of" the group. He later acted as an advisor to the Palestinian delegation during Middle East peace talks.

That was worrisome for many Americans, and in the final days of the presidential campaign, the McCain camp made huge hay out of the tape, and of Obama's relationship with Khalidi, hoping to sway the Jewish vote and many other American supporters of Israel. Fair enough.

But you'd think people would learn that you have to be careful, because when you sling mud, there's always a chance you'll get some on you.

That happened with McCain when it came to light that he, too, had a connection to Khalidi. In 1998, a group McCain chaired, the International Republican Institute, gave $448,873 to the Center for Palestine Research and Studies, founded that same year by none other than Khalidi. You know what? That hardly made McCain an anti-Semite, nor did it seem Obama's association with Khalidi made him one.

I wanted to ask him about that, so I invited McCain's man Goldfarb on my show to discuss the issue, and I asked him: "Now, I need to parse this out as best I can from you, Michael. The fact that John McCain's organization gave $448,000 to this group that was founded by Mr. Khalidi, is there no reason for some to be critical of that as well, just as some might be critical of Barack Obama for being at a meeting with some girl who read a poem, for example?"

His answer: "Look. You are missing the point again, Rick. The point is that Barack Obama has a long track record of being around anti-Semitic and anti-Israel and anti-American rhetoric."

I pressed him.

"Can you name one other person besides Khalidi who he hangs around that is anti-Semitic?"

I knew he was likely referring to Reverend Jeremiah Wright, whose sermons critics say were in fact infused with anti-Semitic language.

Michael Goldfarb was desperately trying to make that link. Barack Obama attended Reverend Wright's church for years and years and likely heard these sermons.

What I didn't know at the time of my interview with Goldfarb was that John McCain had specifically prohibited Goldfarb from mentioning Reverend Wright. It was a nasty association that candidate Obama had deftly addressed with a speech about race in America, which was heralded by most Americans on both sides of the aisle. Bottom line, Goldfarb was forbidden from talking about Reverend Wright, but he wanted to sneak it in anyway.

So, here's what he does. He plays this game on TV with me—a kind of catch me if you can, where he tries to get me to say Reverend Wright's name. That way he could get what he wants without disobeying McCain's orders.

"Rick," he said, "we both know who number two is."

"Who? Would you tell us?" I asked.

"No, Rick," he said, "I think we all know who we are talking about here."

But I wasn't going to provide that answer for him. He had to give me the answer. So I put it back in his court. "No, Michael," I said, "I don't know who you're talking about."

To which Michael Goldfarb just says absolutely nothing.

If you've ever seen a moment on television or elsewhere where the silence is deafening, that's exactly what this was. He didn't quite know where to turn.

So I pressed him again.

It was a verbal Mexican standoff. I wouldn't say it. He couldn't.

Austin Powers, Fat Bastard, and Alotta Fagina may have set the standard, but this may be the second best discussion about who's number two since.

But what was Goldfarb really trying to achieve? He didn't want McCain's inadvertent connection to Khalidi examined. But he did want viewers to say, "Aha! Obama's an anti-Semite. I can't vote for him."

I could see where he was going, and I wasn't going to play a part in it.

■ Why, Oh, Why?

You're tired of that type of politics. . . .

Are they? Who are they? Special interests, politicians, pundits, talk-show hosts who make their money by playing on Americans' fears and stereotypes and whipping them into a frenzy.

Yes, oftentimes it's about race, which can cut both ways, as we saw with the president's defense of Gates. But then there's the word "socialism." That word has been thrown around like crazy in recent years for the same partisan purposes.

The same can be said about those on the left who throw out terms like "warmongers." It is a conversation stopper, a tool used to paint the other side with a broad brush, without taking into account the merits of their argument. It's a weapon used in blind partisanship.

■ Bye-Bye Tribes

The good news is that many Americans are sick of the silly accusations of "socialism," "warmongers," and the like, sick of the blind partisanship, and they are finally getting their message out. Their voices are starting to be heard. I may have been the first to use my newscast as a social media listening post, but I'm now not the only one. And more of us will continue to hear you. We have to.

You tell me—on Twitter, MySpace, and Facebook—you're tired of superficial partisan slogans. Yes, I hear from some on social media who still persist on name-calling. The Democrats are jerks, or the Republicans are idiots; conservatives are stupid, or liberals are weenies. But more often than not, even those kinds of comments can inspire exchanges that are smart, cogent and insightful—from both newsmakers and news junkies:

We need people like you to cut through the BS to get
to the truth that is alien to big business and government.

Yes, point out the companies against any given Bill
and report what they stand to lose.

absolutely yes special interests on both sides have
had too much control over debate.

Some of the smartest conversations taking place in America right
now are found on social media. Sure, there are some dunderheads in
social media as there are anywhere else, but at least they can respond
to each other. Above all, social media is where Americans share and
listen. It's the only medium that is actually forcing a dialogue on us.

By the way, they also tend to be younger than the typical cable news
viewer. The Nielsen research shows that the majority of cable news
viewers are over fifty. So many of the consumers of traditional news, including cable news, tend to be, well . . . older! That means guys like
me are a bit ahead of the curve, but I'm okay with it. I believe my
social media followers and my exclusive TV viewers compliment
each other. The appetite for the social media technology hasn't yet
caught up to the cable-news majority demographic. It will, but not
just yet.

Here's how I see social media, especially Twitter, which forces a
dialogue with short, answerable responses. Imagine being lucky
enough to live in a diverse community where neighbors invite each
other over for backyard barbecues, where ideas are exchanged and different points of view are expressed. Sure there's occasionally the blow-
hard who tries to dominate the conversation, but most people are generally kind and receptive, and share their own thoughts, albeit not al-

ways politely, because they want to guard their place in that community. You can't go to a backyard barbecue every day, but you can exchange daily in social media.

So what is it? Social media is a community, where followers can engage with each other, dialogue—even "duel"ogue—and I bring those conversations into my show.

But it seems to me that the various camps feeding us information often don't want us to be receptive to other ideas. They want us hardened.

Demagogic moments like many of those we see and hear on radio and television are what many of you say you've had enough of. You want real facts, honest debate, and you don't want to look up at the screen and be insulted by partisan rants. Things like that seem to only appeal to an audience interested in neither nuance nor dialogue.

Connect. Connect. Connect. People who aren't connected can only see one side. People who are connected can see both sides and what's in between.

The Great Divide

Those old divisions are causing violent seizures within the existing political structure. The fervid conservative movement is battling with moderate Republicans over the heart, soul, and future of the GOP, just as the Democratic Party often seems to struggle to find the balance between its left-wing activists and its center.

Let me give you some examples. The Democratic Party struggled to find itself during the primary campaign between New York senator Hillary Clinton and President Obama. It was a struggle between the older established Democrats who supported President Clinton and the new younger Dems who supported Obama. Of course, for President Clinton himself, it was personal. His rift became painfully obvious when the former president, as detailed in *Game Change* by John Heilemann and Mark Halperin, said this to the late Ted Kennedy about endorsing Obama: "A few years ago, this guy would have been getting us coffee." Then Clinton went even further by reportedly saying, "The only reason you are endorsing him is because he's black. Let's just be clear."

Here's another example, this time in the Republican Party, where of late the rift seems much more visible. Why? Because some in the GOP are aligning themselves with the right wing—especially as the Tea Party becomes more prevalent.

The first sign of a shift occurred during the fight over the otherwise unremarkable legislative seat in upstate New York in 2009.

The District 23 congressional seat is located in a staunchly Republican stronghold, and was held for sixteen years by John M. McHugh. It came open when McHugh was selected as secretary of the army.

The special election to refill the spot touched off a war between conservative and moderate factions of Republican voters in the district. The party picked Dede Scozzafava as its candidate. But the centrist candidate's support of abortion rights and same-sex marriage upset conservatives. They threw their support behind Conservative Party nominee Doug Hoffman.

The divide threatened to split the Republican vote and hand the seat over to a Democrat for the first time since 1980. It didn't matter. Conservatives were determined to make a point.

True to form, Sarah Palin endorsed the more ideologically entrenched candidate, Hoffman. So did former House Republican leader Dick Armey of Texas and former GOP presidential candidate Steve Forbes. Newt Gingrich backed Scozzafava.

The weekend before the election, Scozzafava abruptly dropped out of the race—and added political insult to injury by throwing her support behind the Democratic candidate.

"In Bill Owens," she said in a statement issued the day after she quit, "I see a sense of duty and integrity that will guide him beyond political partisanship."

Conservatives called it "a betrayal," but nonetheless celebrated her departure.

Who won? The Democrat. Hoffman lost. But conservatives could still declare a victory in the message they sent to rattle Republican Party leaders.

"Our number one goal was to make clear that the Republican Party cannot take someone as liberal as Dede Scozzafava and thrust her out on the voters and expect the voters just to accept it," Brian Brown, executive director of the National Organization for Marriage, told the *New York Times*.

Trading Places

The rift among Republicans had been exposed a few months earlier, when longtime senator Arlen Specter of Pennsylvania stunned the nation by abandoning the Republican Party and becoming a Democrat.

"As the Republican Party has moved farther and farther to the right, I have found myself increasingly at odds with the Republican philosophy and more in line with the philosophy of the Democratic Party," he said as he announced the switch in April 2009.

I asked Senator Jim DeMint to be on my show. The Republican from South Carolina has been a staunch defender of his party's politics, and I wanted to hear what loyalists had to say about Specter's departure. Would he be honest about the loss?

I asked him, "Are you concerned about what's going on in your party?"

It seemed like a fair question in light of recent events, which I went on to lay out for him: African Americans were basically coming out in droves against his party and throwing all their weight behind Barack Obama.

And because of the still ripe immigration debate led in part by my then CNN colleague Lou Dobbs, the GOP had lost much of the ground gained among the country's Latino voters by Ronald Reagan and George W. Bush, both of whom either passed or tried to pass immigration reform to allow illegal immigrants to petition the government for U.S. residency.

So if blacks were solidly against them, and Hispanics were solidly against them, I had to ask the senator to assess his party's dilemma.

Believe it or not, DeMint turns to me and says, "Oh, no, we're the party of the big tent. We're the big tent party."

To which I said: "What the hell are you talking about?" It just came out. It almost seemed like in that moment he was denying the truth. Which was sad. That became another one of those YouTube moments. The next day Jon Stewart went on the air on *The Daily Show* on Comedy Central and blared, "San-chez! You finally said what we were all thinking!"

He was right. And I knew it because it was what some of the people I talk to every day on Twitter and MySpace and Facebook were thinking. They were saying, "Don't let politicians just recite rehearsed lines without being challenged."

What DeMint said didn't make any sense.

That's the point you were making on Twitter that day. You can rebuild, and you can attract followers, but not with empty slogans.

Partisanship and Totalitarianism

I know and grew up understanding why accusations are hurled at certain leftist pundits and politicians.

Fidel Castro has always been a master at scaring the Cuban people and saying, "You know what? You better believe in this, because if not the other guys out there are going to come and get you."

The other guys of course are the "imperialist Yankees," who he insists are going to invade the country at any given moment. I guess we sort of gave Castro that argument with the Bay of Pigs, but that same fearmongering that Castro has been so adept at using to quash his people, making them so fearful that they don't act, that they're essentially frozen, has been used in our own body politic.

That same argument, which is very much a totalitarian argument, has been used by demagogues throughout history—from Castro to Franco, name your dictator. And that same argument is used on all sides of the ideological field. It was put in play by the communists and by their opponents, the people who call themselves anticommunists, antisocialists, antitotalitarian.

For those of us who were born in communist countries or who grew up embroiled in its politics, well, we know that argument very well. I've heard it my entire life. In case after case, I can show you that the people who are sometimes espousing this principle are closer to what I have grown up with, as a child of a communist revolution, than many of the people who they are arguing against.

It goes like this: "We'll get the people to think they are going to be attacked at any moment now. We'll get them really scared. And then while they're scared, we'll get them to go along with anything that we're doing. You've got to follow us, because if you don't, you're helping them." Actually, critics can be both. You can criticize a leader or a political system and remain patriotic, no matter what country you live in.

Some have accused U.S. presidents of employing the tactic as well—George W. Bush during the Iraq war buildup and even Clinton during the Lewinsky affair, the one he preferred Americans had paid less attention to.

▨ Me and the President in My Underwear

In fact, my first-ever national on-air scuffle was with President Clinton. When in 2000 he allowed police to snatch Elian Gonzalez from his family home in Little Havana, it set off a near riot in the streets of Miami and may very well have cost Al Gore the presidency by ensuring a George W. Bush victory in the voting districts of South Florida.

Two years later, former president Clinton's staff reached out to my producers on Univision Radio to talk about the upcoming midterm elections. I agreed to interview the former president on my radio show broadcast throughout much of the country.

They were looking to reach out to my sizable Hispanic audience, and I was looking to force him to answer the questions that I felt no one in the media had pressed him on.

I broadcast my show from my home in Mahwah, New Jersey, which I drove to after completing my morning show on MSNBC. It got both heated and strange. Heated because I pressed him on his seemingly one-sided view of the "Elian" issue and strange because I conducted the interview in my underwear.

That's right. When I got home that day, I heard the phone ring and my wife yelled to me from downstairs that the former president was on the phone. They had moved up the interview on the former president's schedule and I was upstairs changing from my suit and tie to something more comfortable for my radio gig.

I was still in my underwear washing off my TV makeup as I usually do when I get home, when I decided to dash into my studio equipped with an ISDN line, which allowed me to provide a broadcast-quality signal from my home. The studio was across from our bedroom. I dashed there to conduct the interview. It was a bit strange saying "Hello, Mr. President" in my underwear, but I didn't want to lose the opportunity so on we went, though I couldn't help but feel a certain irony in thinking that he had been caught in a sexual scandal during the Monica Lewinsky affair—which made the moment seem almost surreal.

He didn't expect a confrontational interview about the "Elian affair," but that's exactly what we engaged in. I questioned why he allowed the Castro government to seemingly dictate Elian's return and had even appointed his own lawyer to oversee the legal argument. I told him the boy's mother had died bringing her son to America and the father never seemed to argue against it until the Castro government turned him into a "forced proxy for their cause."

Clinton argued vehemently that the boy's father was insisting on his return, but I kept pointing out that he lived in a totalitarian country and there was really no way of knowing what he wanted because he could be imprisoned for opposing the state.

The conversation was heated and it got to the point where we were both screaming at each other. The interview was scheduled for ten minutes, but to the former president's credit, it went on for a full forty minutes. His aides literally had to stop the interview.

The next day I played part of the interview for Clinton's former political advisor Dick Morris on MSNBC, who was then as now a critic of the Clintons and who told me yes, the president enjoys a combative interview, but he also revealed why Clinton was so apt to take Castro's side in the argument. He said, "Clinton is afraid of Castro."

I asked why. He said the bottom line was that as governor of Arkansas, Clinton had been derailed by Castro when he accepted Mariel refugees from Cuba during the Carter administration and he didn't want to do battle with Castro again for political reasons. It seemed a politically motivated argument. One based on his own political fear. That was Morris's take, but he knew and worked closely with the president for years and it was an interesting perspective. It should be noted, so I will, that Dick Morris has since made tons of money on books criticizing the Clintons.

Beyond Parties

We've gone beyond parties. Politics today is not about moving the left or the right; it's about individuals—the ones who vote, and the ones who get elected. The people are speaking.

The old tricks won't stand up to the new technology, or the new mentality. All that the promoters of blind partisanship will accomplish by pulling the same tired rabbits out of the same worn hats is to distance themselves from you more.

But that's okay. Good, actually. Because as they drift off to the sidelines, you will continue to find and connect with more people who think like you, or don't. The point is you'll be able to engage with each other, and the conversation won't end with what you hear being said or written, it's your national conversation.

CHAPTER 2

You're Sick of
Money in Politics

They've got us right where they want us: confused, stupefied, and tearing each other apart while they sit back and reap the rewards. And their reward is millions in moola, if not billions. They're raking it in, and we're fighting among ourselves for the crumbs.

I'm talking, of course, about politicians and the money pouring all over them—to influence the way they vote on things that affect you and me.

Too many of the decisions they make, on big issues and little issues, have stopped being about what's good for us or good for the country. Too many times—maybe even more often than not—it's all about questionable connections, campaign contributions, and potential conflicts.

My dad, an immigrant and the noblest man I know, told me this as a child: "Show me a guy who's made millions and millions in politics or big business and I'll show you a guy who's been willing to step on hundreds, if not thousands, of throats along the way." You'll excuse my dad's cynicism; it comes from decades of hard knocks, which began at age nine when *his* dad passed away. He quit school with only a fourth-grade education and went to work as a shoeshine boy to support his family. Don't tell him about struggling. He's battled every step of the way, teaching himself to read and write and achieve against all odds. He's the ultimate little guy, with a big man's heart, and he's my inspiration to fight on for what's right.

My dad is sick of seeing money and unbridled power in politics. And many of you tell me you're tired of it as well. It's been the same since before my dad said that to me, and before his dad.

> Special Interest groups always influence members of both parties because both parties have 1 thing in common . . . Greed!

> Special interest have too much influence in ALL areas of politics on BOTH sides. Media also too influenced by politics.

Do our politicians care? They should, because what they don't know is that more and more of us are keeping an eye on the money, keeping track—and taking names.

■ A Healthy Example

The first wave in the debate over President Obama's passage of health-care reform is over. But few issues have better served to point out how special interests, and entire industries, use their dollars to confuse and influence our thinking and to directly sway the votes of politicians (I won't say to "buy" politicians, although that's certainly what you say to me on my show).

In some cases, it's blind partisanship. Some special interests are more interested in mucking up the argument with labels, name calling and sloganeering, than debating it on the merits of an issue. What does that tell you?

Take for example the label: "socialist." One of the most commonly repeated catchwords that some have used to try and win arguments, now and in the past, is the word "socialism."

And boy has it ever been used against Obama—by some who hope he'll be seen as even worse than socialist, maybe a Marxist or a communist. The truth is, if you take a clear look at his administration, it would be very hard to make that argument against this president. In fact, you could more easily make the converse argument, as some have, that this president is too tight with big-money interests.

This is a guy who is a Harvard lawyer, who has clear connections to Wall Street, and has arguably taken as much money from Wall Street as any other politician for any one campaign. He is also counseled by aides with ties to Wall Street.

The reasonable question to ask those who hurl such accusations like socialist, communist, or Marxist is, do they not know all these facts?

Here's what you say about the signs held up at Tea Party rallies that illustrated those labels.

I dislike the Tea Party for their lack of diversity.

I LOVE THE TEA PARTY, THEY ARE THE ONLY
ONES WHO ARE FOR AMERICANS; THE REST IS
SUNDAY MORNING QUARTERBACKING.

I like their passion. I disliked hearing them scream in
my ear for 90 minutes during a health care meeting
in Tampa.

Most TPers are good-hearted but gullible & unedu-
cated, being manipulated by hate groups, zealots
and insurance companies.

Health-care reform is an issue tens of thousands of you asked me to look into. You specifically asked me to find out who was coordinating the anti-health-care rallies and in some cases, though not all, orchestrating the rhetoric. So at your behest, I questioned one of the guys behind the anti-health-care-reform movement, a health-care executive who had made millions.

Published reports consistently pointed out that when this executive ran one of the largest hospital groups in the country, his facilities were dirty, doctors were given gloves so cheap they broke, and nurses said they had to treat so many patients they weren't able to handle the demand.

As for the complaints from doctors and nurses about the quality of service provided by his health-care monopoly, he blamed unions for making negative comments against him.

"The unions put these things out," he said, "because they want to unionize your hospitals."

You'll hear more about my confrontation with Rick Scott and how it became a viral moment in the health-care debate in a few pages, but first let's note that there are two driving forces here: the politics and the money. And in the middle stand many Americans who are confused. And the guys and gals loading them with BS on both sides know that, and take advantage of it.

What's Going on Here?

Time for some perspective and common sense, and it means holding Democrats' feet to the fire and getting them to be honest about the fact that health-care reform is going to be immensely expensive, as expensive as any legislative initiative ever. "Why don't you just come clean and admit this thing is going to cost trillions of dollars?" That's what I asked a frustrated and energetic Congressman Anthony Weiner while he was trying to convince CNN viewers how reform would bring down the deficit. Weiner and other Democrats may truly believe the government has a vital role in fixing our broken health-care system—which is ranked thirty-seventh in the world by the World Health Organization. And they may very well be right, but to say that it won't be expensive or that we can do it on the cheap doesn't seem plausible. And most Americans know that.

But on the other side, if you're truly a fiscal conservative, don't you want everyone to pay their share and don't you want a health-care system that makes everybody pay for service?

Ask yourself, if you consider yourself fiscally conservative, what do you want?

Before the implementation of Obama's health-care plan, we had roughly 31 million Americans in the United States without health care. Who was paying for their unpaid bills when they went to the hospital and couldn't afford it? You, that's who.

Here's the rub. Many of you point this out to me, that as a conservative, somebody who supports a fiscally prudent policy, you would say, "You know what? I'm tired of paying for those people. I'm tired of paying for people who don't have health care and whenever they get sick, they just go to the emergency room and they get health care for free. They show up, they get indigent care, and we have to take care of them."

That was a legitimate beef, right? Why wasn't that a major question in the conversation early on?

You have all these people out there who didn't have health care, who were literally taxing the system. And who's paying for it? Well, the rest of us who do pay taxes and hospital surcharges of up to 13 percent, according to the *New York Times*, when we pay our insurance and hospital bills used to offset the cost of treating those who don't have insurance. That's the health-care system, without reform. Millions of Americans getting services without paying for them, while the rest of us paid more. Wasn't that more akin to socialism? Just asking.

You tweet me and tell me you want everybody to pay their own way. Some health-care-reform supporters, who never seemed very adept at selling their message, did finally latch on to that argument. The argument is that everybody should pay into the system. The argument could then be, "Hey, wait a minute. You know what? From now on when you buy a stick of gum, we're going to take a penny of that stick of gum and we're going to use it to pay for your future health-care needs. Or when you pay your property taxes, we're going to charge you an extra couple of bucks for health care. I don't care who you are." That way, I, Rick Sanchez, or Joe in Kansas, or Pedro in Los Angeles, who do have jobs and do pay for health-care insurance won't have to pay for you.

I'm just pointing out what you tell me, that too often we fail to get beyond slogans like socialism and we fail to consider anything else. The arguments we do hear too often are the ones being controlled by special interests. And the American people are either too busy, too tired, or too easily swayed by the dogmatic claims made by the politicians and the corporate interests to really drill down. But you tell me you're angry and you want the truth:

> the movement isn't the issue as much as the message. U R entitled to your opinion, but not entitled to your own facts.

> Too much irrational anger based on ideas that have no basis in reality.

> what I don't like about the tea party is the bad information they are given.

▌ Democrat Anthony Weiner Shooting Straight?

But will health care be expensive? New York congressman Anthony Weiner is a strong, earnest proponent of health-care reform and never misses an opportunity to go on TV and say so. But when he came on *Rick's List* to support "Obama Care," you came at him from two angles. Some of you questioned why he was supporting something that was so "dog-gone" expensive at a time when the country was in a recession. Some of you took a different tack, wondering how he could possibly vote for this version of the health-care-reform bill when he was so adamantly against anything that didn't include the public option. Some of you even suggested he was "selling out."

I asked—no, *you* asked—about both concerns. He responded that something was better than nothing, and then he said this bill would save Americans money and bring down the debt. I knew better than to leave that alone, so I asked what you wanted asked.

"How can you say that? Isn't this going to be one of the most expensive legislations ever? Why don't you just say what it really is, if you really believe in it?"

He stuck to his guns, using the Congressional Budget Office report that said the legislation would cut the deficit by $138 billion over the next ten years. But Republicans pointed out that he wasn't including several add-ons that they said were sure to drive the cost up even more.

Weiner was going by the Congressional Budget Office, but Alan Greenspan, among others, wondered out loud if the numbers were right, as he said in this interview with the Web site Newsmax:

"In other words, in the case now, where our buffer between our capacity to borrow and our actual debt is narrowing, for the first time, I think, in the American history," Greenspan said, "there's a question, supposing we are wrong on the cost estimates, and, indeed, they are actually much higher than the best estimates can generate, the consequences are very severe."

Point is, you tell me you want elected officials to answer the tough questions and you urge me to press them. That's the power of social media.

We Love You, Medicare. We Really Love You.

Democrats say Republicans are being hypocritical by now supporting Medicare as part of their argument against reform.

I brought it up on my show near the end of November 2009, when I interviewed Senator John Barrasso, a Republican—and a doctor— from Wyoming.

Opponents of the health-care legislation were pulling out all the stops as the discussion headed for a vote on the Senate floor. Here's why they said they opposed the two-thousand-page bill.

"It's going to affect one-sixth of our economy," Barrasso said. "And it is going to cut Medicare."

It was a heartfelt defense of the social program Republicans had opposed decades ago but had since embraced.

You ask me to ask direct questions and so I did: "Your party," I said, "the Republican Party, opposed Medicare . . . back when it was created. Now you're arguing for it. At what precise point did the Republican Party become the defenders of Medicare?"

He responded as a doctor.

"Well, you know," he answered, "I practiced medicine for the last twenty-five years in Wyoming, taking care of Wyoming seniors who are on Medicare. And I know what it's like to fight with the federal government for Medicare reimbursements. Medicare is the number-one denier of care. They do a terrible job in terms of coordinating care, in terms of working with preventive care."

It was decades ago, but it still begged the question: Okay, so which is it, Medicare good or Medicare bad?

"But when you're talking about cutting $500 billion from our seniors who depend on Medicare, and you have more and more seniors every day who are going to be dependent upon Medicare, I don't think that the way to solve this is to cut $500 billion from our seniors, because we know that program is going broke. We know it's going to be broke by the year 2017.

"If you're going to do these sorts of things," he continued, "you should do it to save Medicare, not to start a whole new government program, Rick."

It was a fair argument from a fair man who appears frequently on my show. And an argument that seemed to prove that Democrats and Republicans had come together in acceptance of what many believe is a vital social program. He wasn't talking about partisanship, he was talking about facts.

Senator Barrasso is to be respected for sticking to his guns but also, when push came to shove, for shooting straight with the facts when it comes to these disagreements between the parties.

We're in the Money

My research, and your common sense, tells us that when it comes to certain arguments, the money interests often outweigh just about all other interests. And this is one of them. And our reporting shows us that money doesn't discriminate between Democrats and Republicans.

Democratic senator Dick Durbin of Illinois explains it this way: "We're preparing a bill which will be challenged by the health insurance companies, who hate this, as one old senator used to say, like the devil hates holy water."

That's why much of the health-care industry pumped millions and millions of dollars into the fight against the legislation. No legislative argument in the history of the United States has ever been influenced with so much money. They bought commercials, made hefty contributions to political campaign funds, paid an army of lobbyists to work Capitol Hill, and did their best to spread information—and misinformation—to muddy the waters.

The gray often goes out the window when you put enough money into an argument to make it about one group's interests rather than an intelligent conversation about finding compromise for the good of all. And this is exactly what the health-care industry did, by pumping money to politicians, into commercials, and into an online campaign meant to motivate Americans to show up at rallies and town hall meetings. There, arguments were expressed in sometimes illogical terms, including statements to the effect that if the United States passed health-care reform we are no longer Americans, we're losing our country, we're becoming socialist.

Long before the members of the House of Representatives finally voted on their version of the bill, $375 million had been spent to influence the debate. Most of it from the health-care industry. Again, that's the most that's ever been spent in the history of the United States on any debate in such a short period of time.

Now, obviously, if you spend that kind of money to make an argument, you're going to go a long way toward making your points stick.

Some of the politicians who were given the most money in campaign contributions to influence health care were members of the Senate Finance Committee, including the Democratic chairman, Max Baucus.

Baucus chaired the committee that would craft the Senate's health-care proposal. Should it include the public option? That was any variation of a government-run health insurance program as an alternative to private-sector insurance. According to the *New York Times*, 65 percent of Americans said they wanted some kind of public option to compete with the private sector and to bring down the cost of health care. That wasn't a secret. It was published as a result of a *New York Times*/CBS News poll published in September of 2009.

And according to our own CNN Opinion Research poll taken just a month later, 62 percent of Americans were saying yes, they want some kind of government involvement in this system like a public option.

Somehow, when Max Baucus and the other Democratic and Republican senators on the committee put out the first bill, it didn't include the public option. Nor did the final version.

Ka-Ching!

A personal side note now. The thing that makes me angriest is that somehow my profession gets the blame over this corrupt system. Somehow we are the ones often accused of conflicts of interest. Journalists get ranked for trustworthiness right down there with used-car salesmen.

What people don't realize is that if I take so much as a ham sandwich from someone, I have to have a meeting with three people at the network to tell them who it was who bought me the sandwich, why they bought it, and what we talked about.

Most Americans, I think, understand what a conflict of interest is. They understand how it works. Yet there's this unbelievable set of rules for journalists, for cops—for just about everybody—and then there's another set of rules entirely for the guys in Congress, the politicians, and the guys on Wall Street.

That's what Americans are pissed off about. After a while it's just a joke. It's a freaking joke!

exactly! Conflict of interests. Conflict of interests are
writing our laws into congress.

por que son políticos . . . that's the way they are,
don't expect something different.

Ethics have fallen in the ditch Rick.

Nothing new. Why do they run for office? 4 the
percs. They get in 2 office broke & leave millionaires.
Am I right? ubetcha.

Here's an example:

There's this big-name Democrat from Indiana, Evan Bayh, who threatened to vote against the health-care legislation, while his wife took millions of dollars from health-care companies.

You would think he shouldn't be allowed to vote at all, right? He's compromised. How can he be impartial?

Bayh is a moderate conservative Democrat who argued against reform because of his concern about its overall cost for taxpayers. That's fair.

But according to OpenSecrets.org, he got more than $500,000 in campaign contributions from health-care companies in 2008. Okay, fine, a lot of politicians got money from the health-care companies—but, no, it goes beyond that with him.

His wife was on the board of health-care and pharmaceutical companies, according to the *Indianapolis Star*. And she earned $2.1 million in compensation from them between 2006 and 2008. Why did she end up on those health-care company boards? Well, consider this: She was only a midlevel lawyer with Eli Lilly when she got the gigs, but her husband was a U.S. senator and former governor of Indiana. Were they trying to influence him? Those are the questions you tell me to ask.

Most of Susan Bayh's compensation came from WellPoint. It is the nation's largest commercial health insurer and made no bones about wanting to see the public option defeated.

As I pointed out on air, "She didn't even get [the board appointments] until her husband won election to the Senate. What does that tell you?"

By the way, part of her compensation is in stocks. So let's do the math. When Senator Bayh votes in favor of the health-care companies she sits on, their stock goes up. That means his income, and hers, goes up. It's ka-ching, ka-ching, ka-ching. And in any other business, that would be considered a clear conflict of interest. But not for a U.S. senator?

You ask me to find out this stuff and ask this question: What are we supposed to think? That the $2.1 million his wife was bringing in is not affecting his decision at all?

You tell me that's a clear conflict of interest. You tweet me and say too often decisions are all about the money.

> Dems influenced as well Rick, government is fast becoming controlled by the corporation and special interests.

The point you make to me, which is a good one, is clear and simple: The senator should not vote when he's ka-chinging. If there is a direct relationship between his family's bank account going up and the vote he casts, he should just say, "Guys, I'm sorry. I can't vote on this because my wife is on four different boards having to do with health insurance, and I will profit from my position."

In fact, the *Fort Wayne Journal Gazette* calls Mrs. Bayh a "professional board member," having been on fourteen different boards since 1994. But when asked if it influences his vote, Bayh insists it does not. "The reality is I don't even know the people who run the vast majority of her companies. I've never even spoken to them," Bayh told the *Jour-*

nal Gazette. "The reality is, we don't talk about stuff that she's involved with."

He even told reporters that he doesn't allow his staff to talk to people on those boards.

Many of you say you don't buy it. Fact is, there appears to be a conflict of interest, maybe fourteen of them.

You tell me that makes you furious.

Revolving Doors

It's not just campaign contributions or questionable connections that are corrupting our system. Potential conflicts of interest extend all up and down the ladder in government.

One of the biggest problems is the cozy relationship between government and defense. Defense contractors pump money to the guys who are making decisions at the Pentagon. They spend millions, if not billions, on lobbyists and campaign contributions and wining and dining generals and politicians.

Of course. That's what all kinds of big corporations do.

But one of the most outrageous things that you tell me you're angry about involves the "revolving door" controversy. One minute, a bureaucrat is working for the government and making purchases, the next he's working for a private company making a sale to the same office he used to be in charge of, and on and on it goes.

President Obama's first White House Counsel, Greg Craig, goes to work for Goldman. Dick Cheney went from being the secretary of defense under President George H. W. Bush, making $200,000 a year, to CEO of Halliburton, making millions and millions and millions of dollars a year, to being vice president—all in the span of about six years.

That is exactly what economists call "interlocking."

Was he conflicted? Did that make him more apt to make decisions favoring Halliburton and other military contractors because of his ties? It's a fair question. Just as it's fair to ask if the Wall Street connections of President Obama's economic team may conflict him when it comes to Wall Street reform.

So here you have possibly the most powerful vice president in the history of the United States, who, according to commanders I have interviewed, made many of the military decisions in both Afghanistan and Iraq—and you ask was he making decisions thinking as a vice president or as a former defense contractor CEO? And you ask, "Is there a conflict of interest here?"

> Dick Cheney is what Eisenhower warned us about in his speech re: military industrial complex.

> I think of the BILLIONS that Halliburton made off the U.S. govt, Cheney knew it, eventually the world found out too. Outrageous.

> Even if the defense contractors didn't have influence, the "no-bid" policy gave the appearance of impropriety.

> defense contractors have too much influence period. Defense is a government responsibility.

Cheney's supporters say that he did not receive money while in office. And they're right. He did not receive any new money from Halliburton while serving as vice president, as reported by FactCheck.org. But the charge made by his critics is that he didn't need to. They say he was already indebted to them to the tune of two million dollars in compensation for work done prior to becoming the vice president. It's up to the American people to decide.

Private Armies?

By September of 2009, there were more contractors in Iraq and Afghanistan than there were uniformed personnel—194,000 contractors to 190,000 troops. They did everything from run the kitchens and drive trucks to provide translation and private security. That means they peeled potatoes and they toted guns. And, as we saw with the debacle in which heavily armed Blackwater employees escorting an American diplomatic envoy opened fire in Baghdad's Nisoor Square and killed up to seventeen unarmed Iraqi civilians, they weren't shy about using their guns.

It's good work for the companies that get it. And Brown & Root, now spun off from Halliburton and merged with another company to become Kellogg Brown & Root (KBR), gets the most.

According to Defense Department figures, KBR was number one on the list of top contractors in the two war zones, raking in more than $16 billion in just the two years from 2004 to 2006.

Late last summer, disturbing photographs came to light—of what appeared to be drunken, half-naked parties involving private embassy security guards. I invited Laura Dickinson, an Arizona State University law professor writing a book about the privatization of U.S. military and government functions, on my show to talk about what was happening.

"What in the world is going on with our military, where it seems that there are more contractors than there are soldiers?" I asked.

"It's really quite striking," Dickinson said. "It's a huge shift in how we project our power overseas. And this is just one in a long line of incidents of abuses committed by contractors in Iraq and Afghanistan."

The danger goes beyond how big contracts are. As I pointed out during my talk with Dickinson, the contractors have become our paid proxies in the wars, private extensions of our military, but without, it appears, the same accountability as our troops.

"They're the soldiers," I said. "They're like the French Foreign Legion for us, and that takes me as a citizen out of the equation, because it's not a national cause that they're doing, it's a business?"

"Well, look," she answered, "it's getting awfully close to soldiering, and that's why I think we've got to dramatically strengthen the regime we have for overseeing that. We have got to make sure that they can be criminally prosecuted if they commit egregious abuses, just as our soldiers would be."

Of course, as we saw with Blackwater, that's not necessarily the case.

"The reality is that they're there," Dickinson said, "and they're working in our name."

New Rules

New rules went into effect in early 2009, tightening the standards for Pentagon officials. This is how it's described at ExecutiveGovernment. com:

> Among the most significant rules is a regulation barring Pentagon officials who have "participated personally and substantially in a Department of Defense acquisition exceeding $10 million or who [have] held a key acquisition position" from accepting a job with a defense contractor without first obtaining a written opinion from a Defense ethics counselor. The coun-

*selor will determine which, if any, activities the official can
perform on behalf of the contractor for the first two years after
the official leaves government.*

An ethics counselor now can limit what type of work, if any, a
Pentagon official can do for a contractor in the first two years after he
or she leaves government service.

And it prohibits the official from taking money from the contractor until after the ethics opinion restrictions lapse.

Best of all, the new rules aimed the penalties at the contractors.
Any private company caught paying a former Pentagon official before
their ethics restrictions were up risked losing any contracts they had
with the government, and could be suspended or permanently barred
from future procurement.

The new rules effectively double the time limits on existing rules.

Many of you wonder why it took so long to do something that
seems to make so much sense. You say you're angry about this revolving door system—you have a right to be angry.

Haul Their Butts to Jail

Part of the blame for the justice system's failures is ascribed, according
to critics, to the increase in privatizing. We are literally privatizing incarcerations, making it a for-profit system.

Private companies already run jails and prisons all across the country. And that offers plenty of potential to affect criminal justice policies and, as I'll show you in a minute, some sentencing decisions.

Private prison companies typically enter into contractual agreements with local, state, or federal governments that sentence prisoners
and then pay a per diem or monthly rate for each prisoner confined in
the facility. It's pretty simple. If I'm going to pay you depending on

how many people you have locked up, you may have a tendency to do everything you can to make as much money as you can by locking up as many as you can.

Critics charge that the system is set up all wrong. They say it's wrong to pay people by the head to hold prisoners instead of paying them to have some success getting prisoners back on the street, working steadily in good jobs, as contributing members of society. They say if they stay out of jail for a certain period of time, we should call that a success. It would be a system based on keeping people out of jail, instead of in jail. The lower the recidivism rate, the more the company responsible for that would make. Many of you say that would make more sense.

Private companies in the United States operate 264 correctional facilities, housing almost 99,000 adult offenders. Critics say by funding and participating in the incarceration of offenders, private prison companies directly influence legislation for tougher, longer sentences, according to a report compiled by the Sentencing Project. They say the companies running the prisons are in the business of getting as many people in there as possible. Because it's for profit, they are literally trying to stock their facility with people.

The worst example of that would be when people start giving kickbacks to judges to convict people unfairly, or sentence them more harshly so that they'll be locked up. While rare, that's exactly what two judges in Pennsylvania did—to as many as five thousand or more children. Children!

I investigated and reported extensively on the judges on my show. The two, Mark A. Ciavarella Jr. and Michael T. Conahan, took more than $2.6 million in kickbacks from the co-owner and builder of two privately run youth detention centers—effectively to help fill the facilities by wrongly sentencing teenagers to serve time in them.

The families of the kids said their children would have to wait as much as several months in detention before they could see lawyers.

"My son's life has already been completely destroyed," said Ruby Cherise Uca.

Her son, Chad, pushed another boy at school, who wound up cutting his head on a locker. Chad was charged with simple assault. He had no prior offenses. Nonetheless, Ciavarella sentenced the eighth-grader to three months in detention.

By the time Chad got out and went back to school, he was far behind in his schoolwork and soon dropped out.

The evidence against the judges was so overwhelming, they both pleaded guilty; but the investigation to see if others were involved continues.

■ Let's Do the Numbers

So as you can see, these conflicts of interest can take place across the board, from Iraq to Pennsylvania. But let's go back to health care, and take a deeper look at how the influence game is played.

I mentioned earlier President Obama's remarkable record of collecting campaign money from Wall Street, but let's look at campaign money in the health care debate.

Take, for example, Mitch McConnell, a Republican; Max Baucus, a Democrat; and Chuck Grassley, a Republican.

These are three of the key senators in the health-care debate, but how much money did they get in campaign contributions from health-care-related industries? I checked with the folks at OpenSecrets.org to check how much they had received in campaign contributions from the health-care industry.

Well, in the case of Grassley—who once suggested the government plan had a provision to "pull the plug on grandma"—he's received $983,000 throughout his career from health-related industries.

Mitch McConnell—he called the bill a "monstrosity"—has received $1.4 million from health-related industries throughout his career.

And Max Baucus, the Democrat who led the crafting of the bill, has received $1.1 million from health-related professionals throughout his career.

While many lawmakers get money, all three of these guys rank among the top fifteen active members of the Senate in the campaign contributions received from health professionals.

Remember, campaign contributions are the lifeblood of reelection campaigns. As I put it on my show, "That's a big nut for someone who's making decisions about how our health care is going to be run to be getting from an industry that's very interested in how it's going to be run, isn't it?"

> Baucus slowed the discussion down enough to make molasses and stir the attention of many Americans.

> Max Baucus is 'one of those' Politicians who do for the good of Lobbyists, not for the good of Voters. It's all about money.

Senator Bernie Sanders of Vermont is a lefty who once described himself as a Socialist. Now he's an Independent. On air, I asked him if all those people who turned out at town halls and in protests screaming about socialism and death panels should be "just as angry, if not more so, about politicians that are getting all this money."

Sanders was blunt.

"Rick," he said, "you're absolutely right. Look, we pay the highest prices in the world for prescription drugs, far higher than any other country. You know why—do you know why? Because the drug companies pour hundreds of millions of dollars into the political process."

Town Hall Two-Step

As the debate over health care drove forward in the summer of 2009, a raucous phenomenon began occurring across the country. Various legislators fanned out to pitch their positions on the proposals to constituents at town hall meetings, and members of Congress quickly found themselves the targets of vicious verbal attacks.

The first few assaults caught them, and us, off guard, as people began hurling angry accusations at them. They shouted out as the speakers tried to make a point, drowned out questioners, and, more than once, succeeded in forcing the discussions to stop.

Congressman Brad Miller of North Carolina said he got a death threat.

Congressman Lloyd Doggett was chased out of one forum and into a parking lot.

But the disruptions quickly took on an eerie sameness. In meeting after meeting, the interrupters used almost the exact same slogans, in almost the exact same fashion—popping up, flinging their interjections, and sitting back down again just as quickly, time and time again.

Doggett suggested the crowds were being orchestrated. "It's being coordinated—scripted," he said.

I showed video clips that seemed to support his claim. Far-flung meetings followed similar patterns. Protesters shouted: *"Read the bill!"* They repeated the same themes, *"Give us back our government!"*

In fact, it did seem coordinated, and I said so when I went into it, in depth, on air.

"There are instances where you hear people sound like they're reading from, in fact, the same script," I said. "And that's what the White House is now saying, as well. But they're even taking it to another level. They're taking it a step forward. They're accusing a specific conservative health-care executive of orchestrating these protests."

The administration hadn't named the person they were singling out as the puppet-master behind the disturbances, but it was pretty easy to figure out, especially when the White House press secretary Robert Gibbs provided this statement:

"I think you've got somebody who's very involved, a leader of that group," he said, "that's very involved in the status quo, the CEO that used to run a health-care company that was fined by the federal government: $1.7 billion for fraud. I think that's a lot of what you need to know about the motives of that group." The administration was suggesting that the crowds, who were showing up with good intentions, were being orchestrated by someone. And I wanted to know who they were talking about and get him on the record to react to the White House's charge.

That someone was Rick Scott, the founder of Columbia Hospital Corporation, which later became HCA, and who created Conservatives for Patients' Rights.

Conservatives for Patients' Rights was Rick Scott's brainchild and his right, but was he taking it too far for personal reasons?

I checked his Web site; it seemed to be enormously successful. It showed videos of other town hall disruptions, to show protestors what they could, and presumably should, do. It also offered a schedule of upcoming events.

It was very coordinated, and very expensive.

Scott had hired the publicist who ran Swift Boat Veterans, which gained notoriety for a campaign against then presidential candidate John Kerry in the 2004 race.

So I invited Rick Scott on my show.

"Some people have used the word 'orchestrated,'" I told him. "I'm not sure what word you would use. But do you take credit for making sure this is going on?"

"It would be nice to, right?" he said.

Scott's a charming guy. He's good-looking, well-dressed. He's got a nice smile and a friendly manner.

And, to hear him tell it, he was merely doing his part to promote a healthy discussion.

"I think they ought to show up whatever side you're on. You ought to let people know. I mean, we're going through a significant debate about what ought to happen in health care. Show up and tell them what you think."

"But let's be fair about this," I said. "You're not trying to get everybody to go. You're trying to gin up the people who are going to be on your side. I mean, you've got a lot to gain from this, don't you?"

"Well, I believe," he said, "I clearly believe that government-run health care will be bad for you as a patient. It will be bad for you as a taxpayer. It will be bad for our country. But most important, bad for you as a patient."

His critics, however, felt Scott wasn't in it for you—he was in it for him. And I had enough research to suggest he wasn't just a concerned American.

He was, in fact, a multimillionaire investor who was forced off the board of Columbia/HCA because of a fraud investigation. He was bankrolling the CPR anti-health-care-legislation effort with $5 million of his own money and as much as $15 million more from supporters, according to the *Washington Post*. And Scott was still in the health-care business; he owns a chain of walk-in urgent-care clinics.

He was ready to talk, and I was ready to interview. So I brought up how odd it was that he was defending the present health-care system, where he, as a health-care executive, ran a hospital group that pleaded guilty to charges it overbilled state and federal taxpayers and had to pay a record-setting fine of $1.7 billion, the largest in history.

"No one went to jail," he said. "I was never accused of anything."

Point taken. But it sure seems important for people to understand who was backing the fight against the new health-care legislation—especially those passionate folks who had turned out at town halls all across America to defend the status quo. Maybe they might point their anger in another direction if they knew who was putting up the millions of dollars in influence money.

"I mean," I said to Scott, "some would argue, and it would be hard to say they're wrong, that you would be the poster child for everything that's wrong with the greed that has hurt our current health-care system. People would ask, why should they listen to you?"

From then on, it became a bloodbath of an interview. He told me that other hospital groups were also charged with fraud. So his defense was everybody did it.

I looked right at him and said, "You're the guy sitting here telling us that the government plan won't work, that it's screwed up, that it's wrong."

I pressed on, "How much more wrong can it be than what you just described? Not only did your company screw up, but you're here telling us that everybody else did the same thing. That doesn't sound like a sterling system to me, does it?"

At one point he actually suggested to me that $1.7 billion in fraud "sounds like a lot," but really isn't.

I could hear Americans choking on their afternoon meals.

I continued, "Your company was accused of something called 'up coding,' that's where you treat a patient for something minor, but charged the government [you the taxpayer] "for something expensive."

His answer, "I have no idea."

For the record, that was in fact what the federal indictment had accused his hospital group of doing.

I was starting to feel sorry for him; it was getting ugly.

I pointed out, "Your company is accused of going into a region and buying up all the hospitals and then shutting them all down except for one to make that one hospital very powerful, that sounds like it may be a good business plan, but is that good for patients?"

His explanation for doing something like that was that "it was to make sure you had the best equipment and the best employees."

I pulled out two newspaper clippings I'd placed on my anchor desk just for this very moment.

"Why am I reading here reports that your hospital was found to have consistently dirty facilities, doctors who say their operating gloves were so cheap they would break, and nurses say they had to treat so many patients they could not handle the demand?"

The interview went viral and was discussed on the blogs for days.

What I Learned from My Dad

Whatever happened to honesty? Whatever happened to the philosophy behind that old saying "an honest day's dollar for an honest day's work"?

To see such dishonesty is weird for me. Because my dad taught me different.

I hope you will bear with me for a moment while I take a slight personal detour here and tell you a little about my dad, as a way of bringing some perspective to our discussion of honesty and corruption and money in politics.

I'll start by saying my dad is my hero. Not because he's rich or famous. In fact, he has no formal education. None, only up to fourth grade, which was when his own dad died. Imagine losing your father and having to go to work full-time at age nine. But my dad reads two newspapers cover to cover each day, *El Diario Las Americas* and the *Miami Herald*'s Spanish edition, and he has voted in every state and national election since becoming a U.S. citizen.

He came here from Cuba in 1960. He worked two, sometimes three jobs, and even on Sundays until he retired. And guess what? I never heard him complain. He was so appreciative for the "great gigs" America offered.

Those "great gigs" that he bragged about included washing dishes at the Embers restaurant in Miami, busing tables at the Barcelona Hotel on Miami Beach, and delivering furniture for J&M Cabinets out of Hialeah. The last one was the best because he talked Cecilio, the owner, into hiring me as his assistant, but only if I'd be willing to ride in the cargo hold of the truck, if and when the shipments were large enough to require more than two movers.

You want to learn the meaning of hard work? Deliver and install heavy, clunky, and easy-to-scratch kitchen and bathroom cabinets in the constant heat and humidity of South Florida. I knew my dad felt sorry for me at times, but he enjoyed having me around and he especially recognized the lessons I was learning.

What were they? Always do your best. It's okay to sweat while you work. And, don't steal. Because when you do, you're taking money out of somebody else's pocket. Somebody who may have worked just as hard as you do to earn it.

Why do I bring all of this up? Because I feel that maybe that's what the politicians who ignore the conflicts of interest and let the cash influence them have forgotten: They're taking it out of your pocket.

▨ We've Got Our Eyes on You

You tell me every day that you're not going to let those politicians filling their bank accounts get away with it.

Every time I do segments on my show about influence money, you let me know you are paying attention. My Twitter Board fills up with comments like this:

"Thank you so very much for your report about the money that these people get from this health-care legislation, shocking and ridiculous."

And this:

"About time a real journalist stood up and exposed the numbers on how politicians are feathering their nests with us."

Of course, I also get some like this:

"Rick, break some news. Politics is corrupted." Does it have to be?

He's right. We know it. But while that person who wrote that may think we're saying the same old thing, about the same old story, we're not. The words may be the same, but the context has changed. The very fact that that tweet came in during a segment about influence money, and the fact that he felt compelled to speak up, proves that people are engaging in a whole new way now. You're not just watching, you're learning, you're sharing, and you're taking action.

And that's bad news for the officials who want to keep serving the money interests instead of your interests.

CHAPTER 3

You're Sick of the Media Shouting Machine

Think about what you hear on talk radio and on some media. You hear pundits, personalities, and talk-show hosts driving a wedge between us.

Why? Because it makes money, that's why. It sells to cynically aggravate an audience. But in the process it shuts down real discussion.

I bought an old sign on a trip to New York recently. It was hanging in the window of an antique record shop near Times Square. I hung it up on my garage wall in front of my car. That way it's the last thing I see as I pull out before my drive to work. It's a reminder that we've always had someone to scapegoat. It's a late-1800s cardboard print that reads "Irish need not apply."

To be clear, there are very smart and respected thinkers out there on radio and TV with cogent thought processes about the direction our country should take. But then there's the media shouting machine, whose members feed the disaffected whatever they want to hear, fuel their fears with anger and hatred and—as you say—shame all of us.

way too much misinformation and outright lies. Glen Beck should be ashamed of himself.

> Dislike: negativity, really bad information, FOX
> agenda.

What many of you tell me is that you're sick of ranting and disinformation. Knowledge is power, and the more people learn about what's really going on in the world, the less they'll listen to and be swayed by the voices of malice.

Recently, I was asked to be the guest on NPR's show *Wait Wait . . . Don't Tell Me!*, and I was asked a question by host Peter Sagal, a question I hear a lot: "Why are you guys getting beat by FOX News?"

A lot of very smart people who watch CNN ask that question, almost as if they're annoyed that we can't beat FOX. The short answer is, we do.

As I explained to Peter that day, it's important to note the following distinction: While FOX News has the largest share of the cable news audience in the country behind them, that doesn't mean they have the majority of people in the country behind them. In fact, CNN has more viewers than FOX. C'mon, Rick, how is that? you ask.

Here, let me explain. FOX News has more viewers than CNN if you freeze time at any given moment. That's because their viewers tend to stay and stay and stay, watching programs on FOX News, sometimes all day long. But it's many of the same people watching all day long.

CNN, on the other hand, has many more people checking in all day long. So, over the course of any month, we have more viewers.

By the way, good for FOX News, they're good at holding an audience, a big audience; but not the biggest.

> We must cut into the politicos power and use power
> of social media to reach them in real time.

Let me tell you who I want as viewers. There is a huge audience out there that has not been engaged in cable news. They generally couldn't care less about CNN, or MSNBC, or FOX. Or any other cable news channel. They are engaging in another arena—with laptops, iPhones, BlackBerrys, and computers. They tend to be younger and much less strident in their points of view. They are not blinded by rhetoric. In fact, I find they tend to have very open minds on most of the issues I cover. I call them my target audience.

By marrying mainstream media with new media, using blogs, Twitter, Facebook, and so on, I've been able to attract an audience from 3:00 to 5:00 p.m. (EST) Monday through Friday that is generally hi-tech, smart, and free-thinking.

Jon Stewart, on Comedy Central, likes to poke fun at me every once in a while, and sometimes it gets my attention, but he's a damn likable and smart guy. By the way, I also think Bill O'Reilly is a damn smart guy, generally well-read, quick on his feet, and a bona fide journalist. But I digress. Back to *The Daily Show*.

Jon Stewart has a crack staff watching for exactly the kind of thing FOX News did last November in a story about a Tea Party protest in Washington, D.C. The video showed thousands of people attending, but Stewart pointed out something odd in the images.

In some of the images, where there were fewer people in the crowd, it was a clear fall day—the leaves on the trees had already changed colors, and the sun shone brightly in a cloudless sky.

Then, in shots that showed thousands more people gathered, it was cloudy and—strangest of all—the leaves were green again.

"If I didn't know any better," Stewart said on his show, "I would think they just put two different days together and acted like they didn't."

He was right. Someone took video from an earlier event, with larger crowds, and stuck it in the less-well-attended Tea Party story. FOX host Sean Hannity did a correction the next night.

"Although it pains me to say this," he said, "Jon Stewart, Comedy Central, he was right. Now, on his program last night, he mentioned that we had played some incorrect video on this program last week while talking about the Republican health-care rally on Capitol Hill. He was correct. We screwed up. We aired some video of a rally in September, along with the video from the actual event. It was an inadvertent mistake, but a mistake, nonetheless.

"So, Mr. Stewart, you were right. We apologize."

Ouch!

Of course, anybody can make an honest mistake. But twice? Less than two weeks apart?

After all of the flak that FOX took over the first screwup, it happened again some ten days later, in a story about the large crowds showing up for Sarah Palin's book signing. Problem was, they used footage from the 2008 presidential campaign, way before her book was even written.

This time, the network said it was considering "serious disciplinary action" against the editors who chose the wrong video.

But the audience is left wondering, since Palin has always gotten her most favorable coverage from FOX News, could they have tried to manipulate the video to make her look even more popular than she really is? Maybe? Maybe not?

And it's good to know, and good for them to know, in fact, good for all of us in the broadcast news business to know, that somebody is watching. I say kudos to *The Daily Show* when they catch them—or me—on something we could have done better.

Pushing Buttons

The media shouting machine knows how to deliver exactly what its faithful followers want. Both extremes do this, left and right. Keith Olbermann, who like O'Reilly is a capable journalist and smart guy, crossed the line with a wicked attack on Republican senator Scott Brown on the night of his election. Brown ran a damn good campaign. He outhustled, outmaneuvered, and outthought his opponent for the Massachusetts seat that was held by Ted Kennedy for more than forty years. It was no doubt a shocking upset for a Republican, but it didn't give Olbermann the right to call the guy names. Olbermann called Scott "an irresponsible, homophobic, racist, reactionary, ex–nude model, tea-bagging supporter of violence against women." And he once stole a stick of bubble gum, so there! Hah!

Olbermann's rant was, according to the host himself, an over-reach. His support material for most if not all of the name-calling was laughable. For example, his reason for calling him "a supporter of violence against women" was that at a rally a supporter shouted an obscenity about Brown's opponent and Brown seemed to shake his head in agreement. What? What if he didn't hear the guy?

After being called out by Jon Stewart, Olbermann copped to "overreaching." Good for him!

When the echo chamber gets louder, they know their audience will grow. It's business. It's not necessarily fair. It's not really ethical and it certainly isn't objective, but it's good business.

There's a simple rule I learned a long time ago in journalism about fairness. Fairness is thinking before you write or say something about a group or a person how it would affect you if you belonged to that group, or you were that person.

I made a very controversial comment that I've gotten a lot of guff over. I was all alone in New York City after filling in for Campbell Brown. Upon arriving at the Renaissance Hotel on Times Square where I customarily stay, I hit the sack as I usually do with the TV on and the laptop open.

I watched a segment on FOX News that I felt was critical of Hispanics. It upset me. So I sent a tweet that said, basically, that as a Hispanic American, it wouldn't matter how much they paid me, I could never work at FOX and look at myself in the mirror. Moral of the story, don't send a tweet before thinking through what somebody else may say about it.

Boy, I got a lot of criticism for it. Geraldo Rivera slammed me. He went on the air and said I was a jerk, and asked how I could say such a thing.

I didn't mean to insult anybody in particular and certainly not Rivera, who's gone toe-to-toe with O'Reilly over immigration. But I just couldn't help myself from thinking some news outlets seem to pick an audience at the expense of others, and change the facts to suit the audience.

They're not necessarily trying to screw you; they're trying to skew you. They're trying to shift you over into a camp of intolerance, by giving you only one side of the story, or worse, misinformation.

You tweet about this all the time . . .

It gets no worse than Rush . . . he's not only offensive but he infuses race into issues that have nothing to do with it.

▪ Remember McCarthy, Please!

As we look at the current media shouting machine, it is helpful to examine our history. Remember the anticommunist crusader Senator Joseph R. McCarthy. He, like many of today's demagogues, used scurrilous accusations like "communist" and "socialist," among others, to savage a president's administration.

In 1950, McCarthy stepped into national prominence by mounting an attack on President Truman's foreign policy agenda. McCarthy used his committee chairmanship to investigate the State Department and accuse them of harboring "traitorous" communists. McCarthy's appeal was so strong, his rhetoric so vile, critics hesitated to challenge him, because they feared loss of employment, damaged careers, and in many cases, broken lives.

Just as today we see that some politicos would not dare take on some media demagogues, no matter what they say or do.

Back to McCarthy: Not content with just criticizing Truman's State Department personnel, he then went after broadcasters, then the United Nations, and then he tried to zero in on the army. But that's where he met his match.

On June 9, 1954, the thirtieth day of the hearings, McCarthy accused a junior attorney named Fred Fisher of being a communist because while in college he attended a meeting of the National Lawyers Guild, a group that J. Edgar Hoover sought to designate as a communist front organization.

Army counsel Joseph Welch lit into McCarthy, lambasting him with a rhetorical flourish that ended with this crescendo:

"Senator, may we not drop this? We know he belonged to the Lawyers Guild. Let us not assassinate this lad further, Senator. You've done enough. Have you no sense of decency, sir? At long last, have you left no sense of decency?"

And with that the gallery erupted in applause! And the rest, as they say, is history. And so was Joseph McCarthy.

Now to my brush with Limbaugh. Anybody who's paying attention knows that Rush Limbaugh says things that sound divisive. Whether he is divisive, whether he is a racist, I don't know. In fact, my hunch tells me he's not. My hunch tells me Rush Limbaugh is no different from any of us when it comes to understanding race. But his broadcasts, now that's a different story.

That's not to say that Rush Limbaugh is not talented. Or that Rush Limbaugh's not right many times.

I know Rush. Rush and I have been together on a number of occasions in social settings. And there is nothing about Rush Limbaugh that made me think he was any of the things that come across on his radio show. In fact, most of the people I spoke with who were hanging around Rush at that time were under the same impression, that what Rush Limbaugh was on the radio and what Rush Limbaugh is in person are two completely different things.

But Rush says these divisive statements when he's on the radio because, as he admits, he's an entertainer. Many argue that Rush is going to say things that are going to get people talking about the show. Rush is just saying what will bring in the ratings. Many of you call it shock radio with a conservative twist.

The Rush I got to know was pleasant and enjoyable company. It didn't really sound like the guy I've heard on the radio.

When a Gallup poll in the fall of 2009 showed Obama's approval rating above the 50 percent mark, contrary to what other polls showed, Limbaugh accused the polling company of skewing its results by counting too many blacks among the respondents. He didn't cite any sources for his accusation. It didn't matter. Gallup released its poll, and he turned it into a racial issue on air.

Race for Ratings

There have been many occasions when Rush Limbaugh has been accused of saying things that were divisive.

He said during an interview after Obama's inauguration: "We are being told that we have to hope [Obama] succeeds, that we have to bend over, grab the ankles . . . because his father was black."

He calls the president a "Halfrican American" and says his "entire economic program is reparations."

He called illegal immigrants an "invasive species" and, just a couple of years ago, actually said:

"Look it, let me put it to you this way. The NFL all too often looks like a game between the Bloods and the Crips without any weapons. There, I said it."

Of course, Rush insists he's not a racist. He said that he, personally, is color blind. He doesn't see race or think of people in terms of their skin color.

Then why, many would ask, do you spend so much time talking about race on your show? Why is it always an issue worth bringing up, if it's not an issue?

That's the background for the following story about a quote attributed to Rush that I used erroneously and that suddenly turned Rush Limbaugh into Mother Teresa and made me the enemy of some of his listeners. It was a quote, by the way, that had been used by many other periodicals. When word leaked out that Rush Limbaugh was part of a group discussing buying the St. Louis Rams, several players and the head of the National Football League Players Association (NFLPA) opposed it. They said they didn't want someone who made the kind of comments he did owning a team.

In an e-mail to the union's executive committee, NFLPA executive director DeMaurice Smith wrote that "sport in America is at its best when it unifies, gives all of us reason to cheer, and when it transcends. Our sport does exactly that when it overcomes division and rejects discrimination and hatred."

The New York Giants defensive end Mathias Kiwanuka was even

blunter. The New York *Daily News* reported that he said he would never play for the Rams if Limbaugh owned them, and pounced on some of Rush's comments to show why.

"They are flat-out racist," he said. "He jumps on Obama and he jumps on other people for being racist. But a lot of the comments that he said, I feel like they have no place in journalism. It is just an opinion show that should only be taken for shock value. I liken it to *South Park* when I am listening to him."

Of course, in the end, when he was forced to drop the bid for the Rams—after the fallout from his statement about Donovan McNabb being overrated because "the media has been very desirous that a black quarterback do well"—Rush turned it into part of his shtick. "This is not about the NFL, it's not about the St. Louis Rams, it's not about me," he was quoted as saying. "This is about the ongoing effort by the left in this country, wherever you find them, in the media, the Democrat Party, or wherever, to destroy conservatism, to prevent the mainstreaming of anyone who is prominent as a conservative.

"Therefore, this is about the future of the United States of America and what kind of country we're going to have."

But while it was all going on, I told my crew I wanted to do a segment on the controversy during my show. And I wanted to introduce it with examples of things that Rush has said that some of his critics point to as instances of him being divisive.

There were plenty to pick from.

We could have included the instance from just a short time earlier when Rush went on the air and turned a fight between two kids on a bus into an attack on Obama.

What happened was that two kids, a black kid and a white one, got in a fight, and other kids cheered and shouted while it was happening. The next day, Rush Limbaugh goes on the air and plays the audio from the fight and says: "In Obama's America, blacks can beat up whites and they're applauded for it."

Many found that to be a terribly divisive statement. And we could have used that one.

But we didn't.

One of our researchers found a quote reported in the *St. Louis Post-Dispatch* alleging that Rush had said that slavery "had its merits."

The quote was repeated in a lot of places, including on TV, on radio, and in print. But we didn't independently verify the quote.

That was my mistake.

Look, I take full responsibility. A writer helped me prepare a script, and I looked at it. I read the quotes. I asked our researchers and copyeditors about them, but we made a mistake.

And it turned out that quote could not be confirmed, which meant it should not have been reported.

Even the *Post-Dispatch* backed down, and posted a note on its Web site several days later:

"A quote in Bryan Burwell's column Oct. 7 attributed to Rush Limbaugh about the merits of slavery in the United States cannot be verified, and its use did not meet the *Post-Dispatch*'s standards for sourcing.

"Limbaugh said he did not make the statement."

Burwell had found the quote in a book, the note went on to explain, but he didn't name the book in his column. And the book didn't cite a source for the quote, either.

"The *Post-Dispatch* found references attributing the quote to Limbaugh in other publications and on Internet blogs as far back as 1993, but none of those cited a source."

But Rush either heard it on my show or heard that I had said it, and he immediately complained about it. And he was right.

Therefore, because I had gotten it wrong and because we couldn't confirm it, I went on the air and retracted. I apologized for it.

But still the e-mails came in, at least a couple of them every week, from some of Rush Limbaugh's followers, who were appalled that I had besmirched the reputation of Rush Limbaugh with the slavery quote. How could I possibly do that? How could I suggest that the guy who sings about "the Magic Negro" is racially divisive?

It's okay to be a fan of somebody. Rush has very strong opinions and I'm sure that many of his listeners agree with those strong opinions. That's good. But to not recognize that many African Americans and other minorities have a serious problem with Rush's tone? That's like only seeing one side of a story. Your side.

> Rick, you are a repulsive smear merchant, you and all the other smear artists are all alike.

> you slanderous piece of shit!!

■ O'Reilly Showdown

Bill O'Reilly and I have gotten into several nasty public dustups over the years that drew lots of media attention and were often described as "cable wars."

O'Reilly writes passionately about how he felt when he was at ABC News, and how they literally would try to push him out of the way simply because they saw him as not fitting their mold. He is a traditional American and spends much of his show attacking the media for not being like regular people—and to some extent he's right. I know firsthand.

TV news is very much an inside game. It's a tough place for an outsider, and that's the way I felt when I moved up from local news to the NBC network. I was terrified and they knew it. Doubt crept in and I couldn't shake it. Every time the camera came on, I felt like I didn't belong. I was a local anchor; they were big-time network anchors. They were all part of the New York or Washington institutions; I was part of the emigrant, transient South Florida community. My dad was busing tables and working odd jobs and my mom worked in a factory. And, in my mind, I imagined all my peers knew that and looked down on me. As a result, I just had a lot of anxiety early on. That was years ago.

What's Poor?

Poor is eating *carne de refugio*. You call it Spam. We called it "refugee meat." And we learned to use it as bacon in the morning and as an entree at night.

Poor is eating government cheese that came in big bricks that we sliced, shredded, melted, and chopped to add some flavor, and some protein, to our meals.

Poor is living in a ghetto with your mom, your dad, your aunt, your uncle, your brothers, and your cousins—all squeezed into a two-bedroom home full of cockroaches.

Poor is not having enough money to have a Christmas present, and when your parents couldn't afford to buy you a toy—so we got ours by going into the backyard and digging up toy plastic soldiers that other children who had lived there before had played with and left buried in the ground. Mine was my treasured toy to play with when I arrived from Cuba, when I was only four years old.

That's poor.

I remember waiting in line with my mother at the government building in downtown Miami that had a spire that seemed to touch the clouds. We called it *cielito lindo*—"beautiful heaven." It's where we got our food rations and the paperwork that my mom needed to be able to apply for a job.

When we left Cuba, the Castro government wouldn't let my oldest brother, Rudy, come with us. They retained kids they wanted to keep in school and train for the military. Eventually, we were able to smuggle him out through something called Operation Peter Pan. The Catholic Church helped hundreds of kids escape the island by contending they were orphans, and shipping them off to orphanages in the United States.

Rudy wound up in Arizona. And when my mother finally got a job, she saved every penny for three months, so she could go to the convent in Tucson and bring him back.

I remember that day. I was worried because I had never seen my mother go away. She was nervous, too, because she was a refugee who didn't speak English, confused about the way things work here, trying to make her way across the country—alone—by bus and by train. She bundled up all the money for the tickets, and headed for the train.

What happened?

On the way to the train, she was mugged. Here's a woman in a strange country, so poor that she could barely rub a couple of nickels together, and she had finally collected enough money to go get her son, and on the way to the train station they mug her and they take away all her money.

She just sat down and cried, right there at the Greyhound bus terminal.

But here's another reason we love this country. There may be muggers and people who will treat immigrants badly, or take advantage of them, but there are also millions of wonderful, good-hearted people who will help them.

As my mom sat there on a step and cried, the people at the Greyhound station got together and somehow convinced the supervisor to let her get on the bus and go to the train, and they bought her a ticket. She was able to get on the train and get my brother and, finally, bring him back to us, and that's when we were able to really finally start again as a family.

That's poor. That's desperate.

So when I hear someone like O'Reilly or anyone for that matter talk about how growing up middle class with a dad as an accountant is an outsider's position, I think to myself then what's inside? Growing up on a yacht?

A big night out for us was when my dad would load us all into the family's late model Chevy Impala and take us for a cruise along Collins Avenue on Miami Beach.

Miami Beach was part of the lore of being immigrants in Miami. Miami Beach was the shimmering, glittering place with tall buildings on the ocean. It was where immigrants worked. They were the busboys, the dishwashers, and—occasionally, after they worked their way up—some of the waiters.

My dad was a dishwasher. And on Friday nights, my dad would get us all in our Impala and put his arm around my mom in the front seat, and my brothers and I would be in the backseat, and we would look out the windows at the shiny cars and beautiful buildings as my dad would point out and say, "That's the Fontainebleau. That's the Eden Roc. That's the Barcelona."

The Barcelona is where my father worked as a dishwasher and eventually a busboy.

And we, literally, just went up and down the street, driving in front of the hotels with my dad as a tour guide. Then we went home.

We eventually saved up enough to move out of the "House of Roaches," as we called it, and into a place of our own in Hialeah. It wasn't much, but it was ours. My dad kept working two and sometimes three jobs at a time to make sure we had enough to eat, and my mom worked at a factory, sewing the leather soles on shoes. They never made more than maybe $10,000 a year, combined.

In the end, though, I feel that the way I grew up helps me. I grew up among working-class people, and it made me a guy who relates to people, who relates more to the street, who relates more to the barrio. And that's why I've related to and embraced social media, because it's about connecting with people. And that's why I failed at MSNBC, because I didn't connect. And they, being mostly northeast establishment liberals, didn't get me.

I used to think my background made me less than them, but today I understand that that is why I have succeeded at CNN. And that's why people say, "Rick, when I see you on TV, I feel like I'm just having a conversation with somebody. I feel like you're talking to me." Well, in many ways I am. I stopped pretending to be an "anchorman" a long time ago. I just decided I was going to be a guy on TV talking with people.

So O'Reilly and I have something in common. We both have at times felt like outsiders.

O'Reilly: We Ignored the Story?

But just because we have something in common doesn't mean we don't disagree. Boy, have we. O'Reilly went on the air and completely misrepresented the work by me and my colleagues at CNN. When Bill O'Reilly went on the air and said that CNN largely ignored a story about a man who shot two army recruiters in Little Rock, Arkansas, we weren't going to put up with it, and I wasn't going to let him use his shtick to besmirch me and my news organization.

But guess what, Bill O'Reilly? I did talk about it. I spent hours. I spent at least two of my shows addressing it. I brought an FBI expert on to talk about it. I brought a psychologist on to talk about the phenomenon of what makes people want to kill other people. O'Reilly said on the air that the only mention of it on CNN was during Anderson Cooper's show, that no one else covered it.

Well, he was wrong. So I told him so. On air. And at length.

I'm not going to say that Bill O'Reilly lied. I'm going to give Bill O'Reilly the benefit of the doubt. I think that Bill O'Reilly may very well have thought so much of himself that he thought because he hadn't seen it on CNN, then it didn't happen. Maybe he thought, "Well, that's the way I see it."

But it wasn't the truth. We did cover the story extensively.

Social Media Versus Extreme Media

The hyperbole, the divisiveness, the shouting, hopefully these things are all part of a dying old media model.

Social media doesn't work that way. It's hard to do that in a community. There, vitriol rarely wins out. People who tweet, use Facebook and MySpace are much more apt to dialogue rather than duel—because they delight in the fact that somebody else is willing to hear them out.

I think it's the 80 percent rule, applied to people: 10 percent of Americans are on one extreme, and another 10 percent is on the other extreme, but the remaining 80 percent have tons in common.

The old-media model seems to want to make us believe it's the other way around—that 80 percent of us are totally divided. Most of you believe they're wrong.

And hopefully as social media—and the new model of what we can do—brings us together, we will, as Americans, find the middle, and avoid the shouting.

CHAPTER 4

You're Sick of
Mainstream Milquetoasts

ocial media is about transparency. "Here's what I say and see, what do you say and see?" It's not about beating around the proverbial bush. It's about calling things as you see them and then engaging in honest debate. That's a very good trend because it elicits conversation, what I have called on my show the national conversation.

That's why your expectations are often not met when I or any one of us in my profession act like "mainstream milquetoasts."

The Republican governor of Texas, Rick Perry, recently told our Candy Crowley, who now hosts CNN's Sunday morning interview show *State of the Union*, that "Americans are tired of milquetoast."

Milquetoasts! That's when we tread so lightly we might as well not be heard. You tell me you don't want to watch newscasts full of fluff, or read newspapers with page after page on dog shows. Nor are you interested in what J. Lo was wearing last night—although I bet she looked good.

In some newsrooms across America, anchors who only bring you those kinds of newscasts and can't go into deeper issues are called "Bif" or "Bunny." And if they work as a pair, they're often referred to as "Dumb and Dumber." More often than not, they have no idea they even have nicknames, because that would require actually spending time in the newsroom talking to the people who put together their newscasts. These kinds of anchors are rare, and certainly not found at the network level, but you know they're out there.

You can tell a lot about an anchor by simply observing where they spend most of their time. If much or most of it is spent in the dressing room applying makeup and gossiping with hairdressers, uh-oh! Good journalism is hard work; it requires elbow grease, not hairspray. And some anchors don't learn that until it's too late.

I believe that viewers expect the person they see on television doing the news to at least know the news. Is that so much to ask? It's what you ask when you tweet me and it seems reasonable. Be engaged!

Now, I will say this. There is also the flip side. When you come in early and converse with viewers via Twitter, while researching and writing copy eight hours before a newscast, you can get too wrapped up in it. It sometimes happens to me. One has to learn the art of delegation.

The key is to surround yourself with smart people and let them produce, but never stray so far that they can't feel your presence. Political insiders say Ronald Reagan nailed that as president, while two others fell short. Jimmy Carter never learned to delegate and paid severely for it. And George W. Bush may have delegated too much.

Challenging the people I interview is what I do. In the process, I stick my neck on the chopping block, and that gives just about anybody with an axe to grind a shot at me. But again, I wouldn't do it any other way, because that's what you expect from me, and more important, it's what you deserve.

It's our responsibility as Americans to stay informed. And if you honor me by choosing me to inform you, the least I can do is not take my responsibility lightly. By the way, if you're lucky enough to be an American and you choose to not be informed, you might as well get the hell out of here. I'm serious, go live where I was born. Really, go to Cuba. There, you don't have to know anything. In fact, they like you better that way.

Maybe it's because I'm an immigrant from a communist country that I can't stop myself from going after demagogues. Funny how it works, but when I aggressively press a liberal on camera, I'm accused of being a conservative. And when I press a conservative, I'm immediately accused of being a liberal.

I'm neither.

Nor is it that I don't agree with their point of view. When I come out against what my guest is saying, it's because I want him or her to respond to somebody else's point of view, or because he or she is just plain wrong. It's called doing your homework. My job is to find the truth when I can and reveal it, because in the end, that's what I'm being paid to do.

And what I hear from you, every day, is that you're sick of the mainstream milquetoasts serving up the news, while letting guests fling blatant lies and drone on for minutes on end—unchallenged.

▓ Anchors and Mouthpieces

I can tell you this about anchoring the news on CNN: It's hard work. The big three, CBS News, NBC News, and ABC News, broadcast maybe four hours of news a day. Cable news goes on ad infinitum. Much of what is broadcast on the big three is taped; almost everything on cable news is live. When you work at the big three, you have untold numbers of writers and researchers to prepare your material before air and then brilliantly edit it to make you and your work appear completely unblemished.

What Frank Sinatra sings about New York City can also apply to cable news: "If you can make it there, you can make it anywhere." It doesn't work in reverse, though, as some big-name CBS, NBC and ABC anchors have sadly found out—when they switched to CNN.

I've asked producers about why some anchors can't do cable news. Most say the most important quality is the ad lib.

Those are the moments, opportunities really, that define networks and anchors. They reveal you. Because the anchor wasn't able to ad lib, the TV word for broadcasting without scripts, is more often than not why many achors don't work out.

Their work may have seemed brilliant but that's because their work was on tape, and cable news is not on tape.

There is another distinction between cable news and the big three. Viewers! Cable news viewers don't respond to big names. They want content, and they prefer if it's delivered by someone, more often than not, who's got a little gumption. Well-coiffed, pretty readers do not necessarily good cable news anchors make. Stop and think about who the leading ratings winners over the years in cable news are: Larry King, Bill O'Reilly, Keith Olbermann. I think they would all agree, they're not exactly pinup material.

I worked at MSNBC in 2001. Let's go back there to press home the point about viewers. MSNBC made a decision shortly after the 9/11 attacks to use its superstar anchors from its mother ship, NBC News, on its cable outlet. Suddenly, Tom Brokaw, Katie Couric, Matt Lauer, Tim Russert, and Brian Williams began appearing on MSNBC as regulars, while many of us were relegated to the sidelines. Surely, those marquee names would drive viewers to watch and position MSNBC at the top of the heap, right? Wrong! As good as Brokaw, Williams, Russert, Lauer, and Couric were, and they're all extremely talented, they still weren't the right fit. Viewers didn't care for big names; in fact, there was reason to believe they preferred their cable favorites, warts and all, like Chris Matthews and Keith Olbermann.

Why? Because say what you want about King, or O'Reilly, or Olbermann, viewers like even what they don't like about them. They seem comforted by the conversation and they've come to rely on them. Maybe it's because cable viewers aren't looking for slick. They're looking for a conversation that reminds them of the conversations they have with interesting people that cause them to think and learn, not necessarily agree.

The most important skill for a cable news broadcaster is unquestionably the art of listening. It's not easy. In real life, conversations are fluid, you are only focused on the person you're speaking with, there is rarely a limit on time, and usually no one is watching.

On TV, I'm looking at the floor director's signals, my producer's voice in my ear, the clock to make sure the segment is on time, the copy that follows the interview, and oh, did I mention that from time to time I realize I'm on TV from coast to coast?

Me and Bill O'Reilly, Round One

It has taken years to master the art of a live interview, and even now there's hardly an interview I do that I don't wish I could do just a little differently. That's just the way it is.

As it was in 2007, when I was hosting a discussion about a Bill O'Reilly comment that was construed by many of my African-American colleagues as an insult.

After eating dinner at a famed Harlem restaurant, O'Reilly told a radio audience he "couldn't get over the fact" that there was no difference between the black-run Sylvia's and other restaurants.

"It was like going into an Italian restaurant in an all-white suburb in the sense of people were sitting there, and they were ordering and having fun," he said. "And there wasn't any kind of craziness at all."

O'Reilly, who was dining with Al Sharpton, went on to say, "There wasn't one person in Sylvia's who was screaming, 'M.F.-er, I want more iced tea.'"

His explanation made it really sound like he was dumbfounded by the civility displayed by African Americans. Did he really think this way? Could he be that detached, or worse yet, that stupid to reveal himself that way?

In fairness, O'Reilly was trying to make a point that too many *other* Americans don't get to see blacks in that environment, so they stereotype them.

Regardless, I wanted his take, and I wanted to be fair. I picked up the phone and personally called O'Reilly to get a comment from him.

"Hey, Bill, I just finished reading your book on the plane last week, and I often watch your show," I said, trying to be nice. "Now, about that comment you made with Sharpton?"

Bill O'Reilly was not in the mood for niceties!

"Who the fuck do you think you are?" he screamed into the phone. "You better not go with this bullshit story, or I'll make you regret it."

"Bill," I said, "I don't know if we are going with the story—I just want to get a comment from you."

After that it was just one insult, and one vulgarity, and one threat after another. I really could barely hear him over the screaming, and that's how the conversation ended. Did I do the story? You're damn right I did.

I conferred with CNN management, who gave me the green light to pursue the story and analyze it with panels of guests. After all, the show I was doing was called *Out in the Open*, and its mission was to address conflicts created by politicos and celebrities.

For several nights, the blogs and TV writers hyped the newest "anchor wars between Rick Sanchez and Bill O'Reilly." I invited guests to discuss the difference between subtle racism, what many sociologists called O'Reilly's attempt at explaining his dinner, and overt racism, which seemed to be what my guest Roland Martin was referring to when he called O'Reilly's comment stupid.

Then, just as I thought the controversy was on its last leg, it sprung back to life. This time because of something that happened during one of my interviews on the topic.

During a discussion with the author and professor Boyce Watkins, I tried to give O'Reilly the benefit of the doubt by suggesting that the comment wasn't blatantly racist, that he didn't use the N-word. I had suggested earlier that O'Reilly had even discussed the comment on his show with FOX contributor Juan Williams, who is an accomplished African-American journalist with NPR.

"The point is," I asked, "if an African American said something like this, we would give him a pass. Are you going after Bill O'Reilly because he's a big target?"

That is when Watkins went after not only O'Reilly, but Juan Williams as well.

"The fact of the matter is that, when Bill O'Reilly gets Juan Williams, the eternal happy Negro, on his show to congratulate him on his racism, that's like Hugh Hefner getting a stripper to come on the show and tell him that he's not a sexist," Watkins said.

It was a direct assault on Juan Williams, who did not deserve to be called "an eternal happy Negro." And I should have called him on it, but I did not.

After Williams wrote an op-ed on the matter at Time.com to complain, I appeared on Howard Kurtz's *Reliable Sources* and was asked why I didn't challenge the comment. I called Williams a "professional," and said I wished Watkins hadn't made the remark and I wished I had challenged him.

Moral of the story: Live TV is difficult. I had four guests whose fluid, passionate conversation I had to follow. And because I missed one rapid-fire comment, I was called to answer for it. It was a delicate topic, and I didn't say anything wrong. But Watkins did. And I was hit hard by O'Reilly's supporters for it. Now, you know why some anchors double clutch.

But it's a conversation, not a speech. That's what you want. And sometimes during conversations, feelings are hurt. It's the way the game is played.

Fact of the matter is I could have tossed to a pretaped report filed by a CNN correspondent. Or I could have tossed to a reporter who would have shown an edited interview. I could have chosen to not engage in such a raw, emotional topic. But it's in those raw conversations, both on Twitter and on live cable news, that we learn the most about ourselves and our neighbors.

It's Raining; They're Snoring

Here's the bottom line: If I can look out the window and see it's not raining, why do I need to invite someone on television, some "expert," to tell me that it is? I mean, at what point do you just need to look out the window, and say to the camera, "Hi, I'm Rick Sanchez. It's raining." I don't need to say, "Good evening, I'm Rick Sanchez. Is it raining right now? Joining us is Mr. Rain Maker of the International Institute of Precipitation, who says it's raining, and Mr. Sunny Face, of the Clear Sky Foundation, who's going to tell us that it's not."

All I have to do is look outside and say, "No, it's not raining," or "Yep, it's pouring."

> Call it what it is. If more news people would call b-s when they see it, our political system would work much better.

> Isn't it the job of the journalist to point out lies? Otherwise you are just an enabler for whomever shouts the loudest.

> OMG, yes, that was the right tact! CNN has debunked the birthers' claims. Calling it anything else is BAD journalism.

would u present the "other side" of Holocaust de-
niers? There's a point when skepticism becomes
idiocy.

When it's that obvious, all you've got to do is say it. You don't need
to book two sides. When the question is, "The Earth: Flat or Not?"
the answer is: not. You don't need to have someone on the show to tell
you that the earth is flat and another to say that the earth is not flat.
Flat-earthers do not need to be given any heed or mind journalisti-
cally.

Unfortunately, that's what often happens, because some in the
journalistic community have become so afraid of saying the things
that are painfully obvious. We're afraid we might offend this group, or
appear biased against the flat-earthers.

The Birth of a Notion

When I did the thing on Barack Obama's birth certificate, I didn't need
to invite people on to tell me he wasn't born here. He was. I knew he
was.

We might as well do a segment today to talk about whether the
president was born on another planet! Does he have green cheese
coming out of his ears? Let's do a segment! After all, this guy does
have big ears—I'm convinced he might be from Venus. I'm serious:
Look at Mr. Spock, and look at Barack Obama. We must go on the
air and question whether Obama is an earthling. We need to have a
couple of guests and spend ten minutes talking about all the different
possibilities.

Are you kidding me?

That's why I came out that day and said, "Look, I've had enough
of this. Here's the man's birth certificate. Look! It's in my hand. Let

me take you through this. This is his mom's name. This is his dad's name. Here's a newspaper that reported his birth. There is a newspaper birth announcement in there, for Barack Hussein Obama, printed in 1961."

I didn't need experts to discuss conspiracy theories, or to talk about whether he was entitled to be president if he wasn't born in the United States. He was. It's the truth. End of story.

Errors of Omission

If something is flat-out wrong, I'm going to say it's wrong.

What did Winston Churchill say, "A lie gets halfway around the world before the truth has a chance to put its pants on"? Man, is that ever true today.

We should not abdicate our primary responsibility—to tell the truth—and allow ourselves to be used as tools to spread mean-spirited misinformation. Like you, I get angry when I see that happen.

Then there are "errors of omission." It's when we allow the politicians and the executives and the lobbyists and the so-called experts to get away with saying something unchallenged. It's the misinformation that we allow someone to pass on, without us stopping them and saying, "Wait a minute. That's not really true, is it?" It's the silence. It's the lack of challenge. It's the lack of preparation. It's about doing your homework.

News is not about niceties.

If someone on our show says something that's wrong or offensive, it's our job to challenge them on the spot.

I'm the kind of guy who believes that it's okay to tell somebody you think they're wrong—maybe it's because I'm Cuban and Cubans love to argue. I grew up in a community where people raise their voices and scream in histrionic conversations, and then we sit together and watch a baseball game. We don't need to be afraid of challenging each other. We shouldn't be. We have a job to do.

That means holding people accountable. That means making sure they tell the truth. And when they don't, making sure we tell everyone that they didn't.

That's why I did what I did when the president took sides in the case of Professor Henry Louis Gates. Obama is the president, yes. But it seemed he was wrong. And the facts were contained not in his version of events but rather in the police report.

And that's also why I challenged Michele Bachmann, the Minnesota congresswoman, when she suggested erroneous information about health-care reform creating free sex clinics where any teenage girl could go in and get an abortion.

The rules of Congress may allow her to read an absolutely ridiculous and unfounded statement into the record, but those aren't the rules of journalism.

▪ Freedom of the Press—A Responsibility

Sometimes I get in trouble when I challenge my guests. That's okay. And it's okay if I'm wrong from time to time as long as I'm honest about it and I go on the air and I tell people I made a mistake.

I see a big list of corrections in the *New York Times* almost every day that's there just to tell everybody what they did wrong the day before. They want people to be able to trust the information they get in the *New York Times*. So, if they make a mistake, they admit it, and they correct it. That's the way it's done—if you want to be taken seriously, people have to know that you tell the truth and you are trying to get it right. And if you get it wrong, you'll fix it as soon as you find out.

I honestly believe that's what our forefathers had in mind when they put freedom of the press in the First Amendment, right up there at the top, in the same amendment as freedom of religion and freedom of speech. In fact, they put them all in the very same sentence, ahead of things like the right to bear arms. They knew that a free press, dedicated to giving people the truth—or enough facts so they could figure out what was true—was vitally important in preserving our democracy and our freedom.

As an immigrant I understand why. I was born in a place where that freedom was taken away. One of the first things Fidel Castro did after taking over Cuba was to shut down the free press—the newspapers, radio, and TV stations—and replace them with his own government-run media. Why? Because he knew how powerful the truth can be.

So I understand why freedom of the press is so important. And I take it as a real responsibility. I also understand it to mean that it's not about me, it's about you. The media are not here to tell you what to think. They're here to give you information so you can think—information about the things you care about, about the things that affect your life, about the things you're interested in.

We don't use the facts for our own ends. I know that, I studied journalism at a place where they reinforce that. The University of Minnesota's school of journalism is one of the toughest schools to get into. It's a place where they hammer away at the fundamentals: Be fair, be balanced, and as I learned from my libel law professor, Dr. Donald Gillmor, "truth is always your best defense." Yes, we make mistakes, but we try our very best not to, and as soon as we find out that we made a mistake, we correct it.

I am proud to have studied journalism, understanding that disseminating information is a privilege that is given to those who work hard to earn it. I do it, we do it, because of a belief in the principles of good journalism, which involve everything from ethics to accuracy. Those things are important. They are instilled for a reason. And people who graduate from journalism school understand that.

In Defense of an Honorable Craft

I'll always be thankful for everything I learned in journalism school. It wasn't an easy path to get there. First, I had to go to college, which my parents couldn't afford. You know how I got into college? A football scholarship. I wasn't great, but I was good enough. I could run back punts and kickoffs. So I made my way in as a slot-back and flanker. I don't think I would have made it any other way. My parents were way too poor.

While I was playing football at Morehead State University, I won a scholarship to go to the University of Minnesota's School of Journalism, a school that drilled down, more than most, on understanding that the way you gather news is the same for all applications, but the way you write for a newspaper and the way you write for television are two completely different things. There is a nonlinear way of communicating, which is basically the way you write in newspapers, and there is a linear way of communicating, which is the way you write for TV and radio. Linear communication means your audience can't stop and start over again, they get one pass. So you better make it count the first time.

What we do is important. It's a skill that has to be learned. And those who don't bother to learn it, those who try to cheat, those who try to cut corners do themselves and my profession a disservice.

My staff has long discussions every day about the topics that are important for that day's show, and to make sure we understand the facts. First, is it important? Second, is it true? And third, is it fair? We don't just stack it. We ask ourselves, "What do viewers need to know about this? What do we need to say? What's on the record? What has been said? Who is this person? Do we need to reach out to them? What have they said before?"

It's bothersome when I hear people criticize my profession, but I also understand that very few really know what we do every day in preparation to deliver the news.

The Theater of Facts

Is journalism entertainment? You bet it is. And despite the guffaws I hear from traditionalists reading this, it's the truth.

One of the most successful people in television, a guy who knew a lot more about our profession than most ever will, said as much.

It doesn't do you any good to have the smartest newscast in the world, nor the most interesting content in the world, if you're not able to package it in such a way as to attract viewers. Television news is the theater of facts.

Don Hewitt, the guy who created the most successful and long-running news program in history, *60 Minutes*, knew that. And I learned it from him when I was just a boy watching television in Hialeah.

I was a product of TV, growing up in the 1970s in the United States. I used to love to watch everything on TV. And I remember one day, I was probably in junior high, when I looked up and saw Phil Donahue interviewing Don Hewitt.

At one point, Phil Donahue asks this man who is such an icon in television, one of the inventors of the newsmagazine format, "Is TV news entertainment?"

Donahue let the words out slowly, almost as if he was ashamed to ask it, as if he was afraid. It seemed like he expected Hewitt to say, "No way in hell!"

Instead, Don Hewitt, who was memorialized when he died last year as one of the greatest broadcast journalism thinkers and producers ever, looked at Phil Donahue and said: "Hell, yes, it's entertainment! That's what we do. We entertain people with news. And anybody who denies that is crazy."

That stuck with me. I was just a kid, but it made a lasting impression.

Too many purists don't understand this, even though one of the greats in the news industry, Don Hewitt, did. And those who deny that news is entertainment set themselves up for their own demise as a result.

"Four words," Hewitt would say, "tell me a story." If you're not a good storyteller, if you can't use words to draw people in, then you might as well just sit there and read numbers at them. That's about as much impact as you're going to have.

> TV news is always entertaining and thought provoking. It either makes me laugh, angry, interested, disgusted or happy.

> If it is enlightening and thought provoking, I suppose it could be entertaining.

There is a disconnect between real people and most journalists. We shouldn't talk at people, we should talk with them. That's one of the reasons I turned to social media and was the first to turn my newscast into a conversation. I was noticing that people were starting to go away. I didn't exactly understand why, then; but I knew that I had come up with an answer to be impactful, to really talk to people the way people talk with each other.

Here's the takeaway. Good journalism doesn't have to be a choice between vanilla and vitriol; both are losers.

◼ The New "New Journalism"

So what do we have? The mainstream milquetoasts among us are putting viewers to sleep. The media shouters are undermining the credibility of news. One is stuck on the ever-shrinking outposts of tradition, disappearing into a sea of indifference. While the other, the shouters, may be destined to become victims of their own debauchery. And you are telling me you'd like to see both of them out of work.

You say you want the journalistic model to change. You don't want to be read a list of stories. But you also don't want to have opinions shoved down your throat. And most of all, you want to be engaged and involved.

Those of you who watch the news as a three-screen experience, with a TV, a laptop, and a cellular phone close at hand, tend to absorb the news. And you tend to be younger.

Given the trend, over the next ten, twenty years, it's precisely that audience, that demographic, who may dominate as news consumers, and that's a good thing. Hell, I see it in my own kids. I have four, but the two older ones have taught me more than they know. Ricky is a twenty-year-old sophomore at Florida International University in Miami who gets his news mostly from his iPhone and augments it occasionally with CNN. Robby is a senior in high school who lives on his laptop, sponging any interesting bit of information he can find. He also watches CNN, mostly to make the ol' man feel good.

What is added by doing a newscast that engages people on social media? Here, let me explain. When viewers like, let's say Fran and Mike, see me on TV, I'm a guy in a suit in a faraway studio surrounded by lights and cameras. But when I follow and respond to people on Twitter or I use their posts on my show, or even just respond to general tweets in their discussion groups, I shrink the virtual distance between them and me by miles. It's a kinship. It's not an abstract relationship, it becomes much more personal. And it multiplies exponentially, which means they and everybody they associate with is now a part of my community, our community.

So, five or ten years from now, looking down the line, social media communities like ours will only continue to grow and grow. It's the new thing and it's here to stay. So while we may look out now across the cable news horizon and see mostly older, and in many cases angrier, viewers, eventually those folks will be replaced by the next generation of viewers, who appear to be much more informed and accepting.

■ The Old Model

Look, I know you've got plenty of places where you can find out what's happening. You tell me you like the fact that I call 'em as I see 'em and that I'm not afraid to go in and mix it up a little bit with the guests. You wanted a place where people wouldn't just be allowed to say whatever they wanted; they'd have to explain and defend themselves. You wanted news with perspective and smart analysis that you would be able to take part in. And you want us to go after the truth and call out those who try to deceive, even if it's my competition.

What? Even if it's the competition? Now, that can be dicey. And it did get dicey—especially on the day I took on the entire FOX News Network and told them I wasn't going to let them get away with saying whatever they wanted unchallenged anymore.

That is not something anchors usually do. I did, with management's blessing. Here's part of what I said.

"There is something that I have to tell you now. If you watch this show every day, as I mentioned a while ago, you know that I usually don't suffer fools gladly, especially when it comes to the fools who perpetuate falsehoods.

As I spoke, I noticed that behind me in the world headquarters of CNN, right there on the fifth floor, it started getting real quiet. Every single writer, researcher, producer, editor, supervisor, even the maintenance people put down their tools and turned up the volume on their monitors.

I continued, explaining to viewers about the full-page ad FOX News had taken out in that day's *Washington Post*.

"FOX News's full-page color ad today," I said. "It asks: 'How did

ABC, CBS, NBC, MSNBC and CNN miss this [story]?' They're referring to the picture there of the Tea Party protest in the nation's capital last Saturday. They are saying that we missed this story. They are saying we did not cover this story. They are using a lie to try and divide people into camps—and, you know, Americans are starting to get tired of this."

As I sat on the main set and lit into FOX News, just to my right I was able to catch the movements of the international desk, where people are talking about euros and oil and diplomatic tensions with correspondents in all the different CNN bureaus all over the world, in all different languages.

Let me describe the rest of that historic newsroom from where wars, disasters, and elections were first reported. Behind me are the members of the illustrious row of editors who review all CNN scripts. Farther to my right are the video editors who take in feeds from bureaus all over the country. And then just behind them are the folks who work the phones and stay in constant contact with the national bureaus in places like Denver and Dallas and Miami.

All these people work together in a vibrant atmosphere. And they are noisy. I don't really hear it when I'm anchoring anymore because I've gotten used to it, but between the intercom, the phones ringing, and the loud conversations, it can seem like a huge distraction to an outsider.

I was well into my litany against FOX News when I began to realize that what was actually distracting me was the lack of noise. It was eerily quiet and I wondered, "What the hell is going on?"

But I wasn't going to stop now. FOX News was wrong. They had lied. We did have correspondents all over that protest, and we covered it repeatedly, throughout the day. I had proof, on video. So I asked director Roger Krause to roll it—clip after clip: Kate Bolduan, Fredricka Whitfield, Lisa Desjardins, Don Lemon, Jim Spellman.

I even showed a clip from Bill O'Reilly's show on FOX itself, talking about our coverage and showing a clip from our newscast! How can FOX News accuse us of not covering an event they showed us covering? What are they, blind?

I was just getting started, and the newsroom knew it. You could have heard a pin drop. I was actually hearing my own echo for the first time ever, as the sound of my voice bounced back at me from all the monitors turned up across the newsroom.

"Let me cut to the chase," I concluded. "When thousands of Americans showed up at the nation's capital to protest big government, we covered it with four correspondents, two satellite trucks, multiple live interviews, lawmakers on the record, and conversations with attendees.

"By the way, we put a call into FOX News for a comment, and we expect an apology. But we're still waiting.

"Let me address the FOX News Network now perhaps the most current way that I can, by quoting somebody who recently used a very pithy phrase. Two words. It's all I need—'You lie . . .'"

I was referring to the phrase used by South Carolina Republican congressman Joe Wilson, "You lie," at President Obama while he was addressing a joint session of Congress. They got it.

At the very end, I stopped and I looked at the camera, and the director then faded to black, and we went to a commercial. And as he faded to black, I started hearing someone clapping, slowly. Then another. And then another. And then the room started filling with people standing and applauding.

I was embarrassed. It seemed the entire CNN world headquarters newsroom was on their feet. It's as if I had lifted some burden off their backs, by saying what so many in that room had wanted to say for some time.

That's what they said afterward. They had waited, some in the room told me, for somebody to come out and tell it like it is. It was a good day.

CHAPTER 5

You're Sick of
Wall Street's Greed

The economic meltdown served as a bitter example of what we should have known all along—as I like to say, when you let the foxes run the henhouse, the chickens get slaughtered. Wall Street's greed shouldn't come as a surprise to anybody; and the fact that leaving the financial institutions unchecked led where it did shouldn't, either.

But, boy, talk about a group of people who just don't get it: When the auto executives came begging for handouts from Washington—billions of dollars from the American taxpayers—they flew in corporate jets. Are they kidding?

Sadly, they weren't. Sadder still, insiders tell us we couldn't just say no. Because, as they put it, "if they go down, we all go down." And the fact is, they aren't the only ones responsible for this mess. Everybody got greedy—Detroit, Wall Street, and Washington. And we all pay.

It's really not that complicated: They gambled, we lost. They found ways to play with our money until in some cases it wasn't worth anything anymore. We sent our jobs overseas. We became a nation that got better and better at running things, but we stopped making things. We got trapped in a vicious cycle that seems like a contradiction in terms: We wanted things cheaper and cheaper, until we couldn't afford them anymore; and the poorer we got, the more we bought.

EVERYONE responsible. All reaped the rewards but
no one wants to be held accountable for contributing
to the meltdown.

as a culture we have come to accept an anesthe-
tized reality in which we are constantly being sold
something.

It is true that Americans—as you tell me every day—are sick of
Wall Street's greed, and sicker still that we had to bail them out after
they got in trouble. It seems like they're not being punished, they're
being rewarded.

But it is also true that all of us acted like a bunch of kids let loose
in a candy shop. It's not pleasant to think about, but the reality is we
gorged ourselves like gluttons until we made ourselves so sick we
wanted to puke.

You know what I'm talking about. You think our homes refi-
nanced themselves? You think those credit card balances and credit
lines slipped under the door on their own? Or was that Wall Street,
too? They put the plasma TV in the living room? The swimming
pool out back? The new car in the driveway?

Who are we kidding? We're sick at the idea that we might be
guilty in all of this, too. Even if you didn't refinance, or overspend,
you still may have played a role. How? Were you the business owner
who extended credit? Or who let that couple put that new furniture
on their credit card? Did you sell them the car or the TV?

Are you guilty? Maybe. Sick? Definitely.

But here's a thought that might make you even sicker:

We may not like it, but the truth is, if you turn us loose we'll likely
do it again. So, as much as we don't like it, we need some adults to set
some limits as we do with our children. Without rules, we—and Wall
Street—will just do it all over again.

▨ Beggars in Private Jets

Consider this:

In late September 2008, the CEOs of the big three auto companies—Ford, Chrysler, and GM—traveled to Washington to ask Congress for a bailout. Because they appeared to be only plugged into the "old model," they didn't know of a condition I had talked about on the air that week: "bailout fatigue." The economy was in the dumps, and Americans were sick and tired of hearing from big companies like J.P. Morgan, Goldman Sachs, Merrill Lynch, Freddie Mac, AIG, and others getting billions of dollars to save them from the mess they were responsible for creating in the first place.

These big three auto CEOs were so clueless, so engrossed in their own stuffed-shirt world, so disconnected, they made fools of themselves.

From my vantage point, it was like watching a train wreck. You see, I learned about "bailout fatigue" because I sensed the mood on social media. I was hearing it daily from the tens of thousands of angry Americans I connect to on Twitter, MySpace, and Facebook. I knew the frame of mind out there. I knew what the auto execs were heading into. But they didn't know, because they weren't connected to anyone other than perhaps their midlevel yes-men.

> i'll be there in a few . . . my private plane ya'll paid for
> just landed.

> People w/$ don't associate themselves w/ reality.
> They live in a world that caters them. So the little
> people should give them $$.

The train wreck came in the form of three million-dollar corporate jets that flew the three unsuspecting, unknowing, and disconnected CEOs right into the . . . *Crash!*

There they were, the heads of Ford, Chrysler, and GM, at a hearing of the House Financial Services Committee, asking for a $25 billion loan of taxpayer money—while the economy is in a meltdown and American workers are being laid off all across the country. They wanted those same American people to reach into their pockets and rescue them, and yet they still get to fly in private jets.

Democratic representative Brad Sherman of California was classic. He asked the three auto execs to "raise their hand if they flew here commercial."

Nobody moved.

"Let the record show, no hands went up," he said. "Second, I'm going to ask you to raise your hand if you are planning to sell your jet in place now and fly back commercial."

Again nobody moved.

"Let the record show," Sherman said, "no hands went up."

How could the nation's top auto executives be so clueless as to arrive in D.C. claiming to be broke and asking for handouts, aboard $1 million corporate jets? They could have flown commercial—hell, they could have flown first class, or shared a ride on one jet if they had to. But three separate trips estimated to cost more than $90,000, while begging for a bailout?

They didn't stand a chance. They didn't connect and they paid dearly for it.

But they were just three more examples of what by then seemed to be standard operating procedure at the big corporations.

One automaker distinguished itself by rejecting the government money. "I think we're very much respected for . . . running a healthy business and not asking for taxpayer money," Ford CEO Alan Mulally told reporters.

Ford won praise and brand recognition for going it alone, not to mention financial success. By early 2010, Ford had increased its share of the U.S. market and seen its stock increase six-fold over the last year and was hiring workers in a recession.

But the other two automakers found themselves at the mercy of a government dole-out and the economic meltdown that had begun a year earlier, though eventually they too began to turn the corner.

The Train Had Left the Station

The truth is, for the automakers and most of the titans of industry, the train wreck had been coming for almost three decades. The same rules that may have created the boom years of the '80s and '90s may have also propelled the meltdown of the last couple years, according to many of the financial experts I interviewed.

The seeds of the crisis were planted almost thirty years earlier during the Ronald Reagan administrations and continued flourishing through presidents Bush, Clinton, and Bush again, and the jury is still out on how it will continue during Obama's. Many economists say it was born of a simple philosophy based on a love of free markets, which led to the lifting of regulations that were meant to protect us but were seen as hindering the potential of business.

Deregulation began with the idea that big government was stifling economic growth. That meant the rules and regulations that stifled business stood as obstacles to that ideal, and therefore should be reduced.

At its most extreme, that free enterprise philosophy could best be summed up in the words of the character Gordon Gekko in the movie *Wall Street*: "Greed is good." Director Oliver Stone, of course, believed just the opposite and was obviously trying to wave a warning flag.

Reagan's fundamental belief was that what was good for business would be good for the country. And it worked for several decades. The country did rebound from the stagflation years of the '70s. Was deregulation meeting its expected outcome? It certainly seemed so at the time. Here, just look at the numbers.

From 1983 to 1989 we experienced six consecutive years of economic prosperity. And during the Clinton years, 16 million jobs were created while we lived through one hundred months of economic expansion.

But there were legitimate questions even back then about the national debt, and there's the question of deregulation. How much? That is a big part of this story. But first let's talk about us.

The Gospel of Prosperity

Eventually, some people's love of the almighty dollar even permeated religion.

A strange phenomenon happened over the last fifteen years or so in this country. Some traditional churches and their parishioners bought into and began preaching about what it called the gospel of prosperity. The gospel of prosperity is an ideology where people think that by getting rich they are serving the Lord. Somehow, in their minds, there is a connection between making money and doing God's work. So, by getting rich, they are serving the Lord!

It's crazy, but that's what they believe. I mean, you've got Jesus himself saying it's easier for a camel to pass through the eye of a needle than it is for a rich man to enter the kingdom of heaven, and here on Earth, people who say they believe in him and follow his ways are telling us that what he really meant was the more we stuff our pockets full of cash, the better Christians we are. What?!

Well, no! That's not what Jesus said.

It seemed they changed the rules. I interviewed Creflo Dollar, who was telling his followers, basically, that the Lord is happy when your bank account is full. Creflo Dollar is a minister who has thousands of people who come listen to him preach and point to passages of the Bible, like "The Lord takes pleasure in my total life prosperity" (Psalm 35:27), as proof.

And then, of course, as soon as they make money, or even if they don't, they are asked to give money to the church so that they can continue to preach to get other people to make more money. You have some—not all, maybe few comparatively—well-known ministers in the United States who wore $3,000 suits. They flew in private planes. They bought Rolls-Royces and drove them to church. Even if they were few, it was enough to outrage our audience when I aired my report on it. Here's what you told me:

"Jesus was modest. You are not."

I'm indifferent about "prosperity gospel" but I'd like to know if people think that all preachers are supposed to be poor.

jesus would drive them out with a bullwhip and then blow up their bentley's with a magic fireball.

I say Just b/c the lord is my Sheppard that doesn't make me a sheep. Open your eyes!

God warned to beware of false profits, just forgot 2 add "that pick your pocket!!"

And some Americans—people who are part of a country that was once built on values, on teamwork, on sticking together, on helping the little guy, on helping your neighbor—wondered out loud if the earnings and spending habits of these ministers were right. Was it right? You generally say no. But, as the philosophy of "money is king" took hold, the ideology of many of our institutions seemed to be turned on its head. People somehow got so screwed up. It permeated our business system, it permeated our government, and it permeated religion—and it may very well have been, as many experts have noted, the underpinning of our current economic crisis.

But couldn't we argue that it's not just about our financial crisis? Isn't it fair to ask if we ourselves may have lost our way?

Cheaper Till We're Broke

I mean, it's this bizarre irony, if you think about it.

We used to have thriving little towns all over America where people had their shopping area with their little hardware store, and a clothing store, and a pharmacy, and a little grocery store where they sold local goods that were produced within the community.

But suddenly we were all about superstores, and superlarge auto dealerships, and supersized just about everything else.

Were we putting too much emphasis on making things less costly at the expense of quality?

Auto industry experts I have interviewed point to Detroit as the glaring example of this. At first, the Japanese beat the United States on price. And when the American automakers tried to compete there, the Japanese still won. They offered a quality product. It resulted in many American car buyers who used to choose Lincolns and Caddies instead buying Lexus and Infiniti.

Here's the irony: Auto experts like Rick Newman of *USA Today* tell me that when it comes to quality, Detroit caught up with and even surpassed their foreign competitors. And now the story may be turning on its head, with Toyota saying it may have overproduced and hurt its brand. That was part of their response to their battle to undo the costly brand damage from the "unintended acceleration" nightmare they faced this year.

■ Superstores

When we think of the new American business model, we all think of superstores like Walmart. And we celebrated their collective successes. Businessmen studied it and tried to repeat it. It was the epitome of the American business ideal, at least at the time. Again, the ideology was, if you came up with a good plan, you should be able to do it, and no one in the government should prevent it.

Now, some social psychologists and sociologists are asking if it's good. Is the superstore model good for America? Fair question, but there are two good sides to this story.

There are those who argue that superstores can sell things inexpensively because many of the workers who are making their products are working in sweatshops. CNN has reported on that revelation extensively, but the stories have never quite had the impact on viewers that some might expect. We've all found ways to care about it, but not so much.

The fact is superstores have become part of the American fabric because they allow moms and dads trying to make ends meet to shop for their kids and for themselves. They allow the elderly to make do on fixed incomes.

Most Americans have benefited, but some wonder, at what cost?

■ The House That Gordon Gekko Built

The economy that we created over the last forty years was no doubt a benefit to many Americans, even if it was based on a relative short run.

But a lot of Americans jumped in and got in over their heads. It wasn't just the executives in the big banks or the auto company CEOs jetting around in their private planes.

Americans did it during the tech boom, pumping their money into overinflated stocks, ignoring the risks as the market soared higher and higher. Nobody wanted to listen to a stick in the mud like Alan Greenspan talk about "irrational exuberance."

Then the bubble burst, and people all across the country saw their life's savings wiped out. Then they wanted to know why the government hadn't protected them. Why hadn't Washington, or someone, prevented them from putting their hard-earned dollars into what turned out to be little more than a sophisticated spin of the roulette wheel?

Before we pushed too hard on that front, and before we made any real progress to keep the same thing from happening again, we got distracted. That gold mine might not have panned out, but the rush was on for another one. Suddenly, people all across the country—not just big banks and wealthy speculators, but average folks—were sinking their money into real estate. That's where the easy money could be made.

The housing market boomed, and people pumped their money into overinflated properties, ignoring the risks as the prices soared higher and higher. What could go wrong? This was nothing like the tech stock boom.

Until it was.

All through those years, we continued to lead ourselves into this spot, but as long as we were all putting money in our pockets, we didn't think about it so much.

One of the reasons experts say the housing market is in so much trouble is not just because of regular folks buying homes that they could barely afford or not afford. It's because of a bunch of speculators who kept saying someone else will buy this. It was inflating the stock price. Only now, the stocks were homes. And then, the thing that took it from crisis to catastrophe was that those same banks that were providing the money for people to gamble on houses created bizarre and complicated ways to gamble on the mortgage notes themselves.

It was like the casinos were gambling with the players' money before they even laid down their bets.

Off with Their Rules!

Of course, it wasn't just our "irrational exuberance" that led us here. We needed Washington's help opening the gate so we could get down the road to ruin.

We'd been there before. We had seen what loose rules and no rules in business could lead to. That's why, after the Great Depression, rules and regulations were put in place to keep what happened then from ever happening again. These were the ground rules that made the world envy our economic banking system and our sense of fair play, discipline, and organization.

But along came the free-market thinkers, who, perhaps with good intentions, started us down a path toward the brink of collapse. Pragmatic and concrete banking regulations that came about from the financial collapse of the Great Depression were systematically dismantled. While this steady push for deregulation began in 1982, it actually continued through the very last year of the century, 1999.

In effect, we shredded the safety net. Then we went out to swing on the trapeze.

It could not have been more obvious what the plan was. Presidents

Bush, Clinton, Bush, and going all the way back to Reagan all seemed to favor deregulation. So much so that Ronald Reagan's first treasury secretary was the former CEO of Merrill Lynch. And he also made himself chairman of the Depository Institutions Deregulation Committee.

In 1982, Treasury Secretary Donald Regan ushered through the Garn–St. Germain Depository Institutions Act, which got rid of the barriers on the savings and loan industry. The barriers were there for a reason, we would later find out, and as I discovered on the air talking to leading economists.

What the 1982 act allowed savings and loans to do was act like regular banks by making commercial, corporate, and business loans of up to 10 percent of their assets. But since the Great Depression we had tried to make sure that didn't happen by keeping them apart and separate. But the Garn–St. Germain Act would begin eroding that separation until finally it led, according to economic historians, to the S&L scandal and collapse.

But that was just the beginning.

Some economists say the most important act of deregulation that eventually led to the subprime meltdown was the elimination of the Glass-Steagall Act. It was there to prevent the banking industry from speculating with the money in our savings accounts. Its elimination in 1999 under President Clinton opened the way for commercial banks and investment banks to merge.

Critics say that allowed them to work both ends against the middle. They could offer mortgages to people buying homes, then whip up complicated investment schemes that they could sell on Wall Street. And when the payoffs started rolling in, they got drunk on the profits. If a little is good, then more had to be better. To sell the investment schemes, they had to sell mortgages. And when they ran out of good, solid, financially secure home buyers to sell mortgages to, they concocted cheap and increasingly risky financing plans so they could sell to the rest—the subprimes, as they are known.

Then, in 2004, the final piece clicked into place. Economists say it was a little-noticed ruling by the Securities and Exchange Commission, reducing the amount of cash reserves that investment banks were required to keep on hand.

In 2008, history repeated itself as the pro-business, antigovernment, and to hell with FDR's New Deal philosophy that took over our politics from the Reagan years through Bush and Clinton and the "W" years caught up with us.

▎Funny Money

Along the way, it all got so complicated that it's hard for people like you and me to understand.

Experts tell me deregulation allowed the financial wizards on Wall Street to come up with schemes that were little more than phenomenally complex shell games. They moved money from one place to another, making every bank think they were the only one with the money, or as it turns out, the only one with the debt, under their shell. Eventually it ended up being more like a game of financial Russian roulette, devised by some really smart and tricky guys who figured out a way of making money for hedge funds by making side bets on all the debt that was being accumulated on mortgages.

Naturally, the more mortgages out there, the more money these guys stood to make, so soon enough we ended up with things like no income verification, no money down, interest-only, adjustable rate mortgages. Armed with snake oil like that, banks not only *allowed* people who couldn't afford a $100,000 home to buy a $500,000 one, they encouraged it.

How could they do it? Because the money wasn't in the mortgage, the real money was in things called credit default swaps. So curious was I on this subject that I spent weeks on my show drilling down on this phenomenon with physicists, economists, and anybody else who could better explain it to us. It was conceived by mathematicians, so I called on mathematicians to explain it to you. Here's how it was explained. Companies like AIG swapped their credit rating for easy money. They insured what turned out to be bad loans over and over again. And since they had an A rating, by lending their name to the loans, they made all the loans they insured look good. The pension fund making the loan looked good, the company getting the loan was happy, and AIG's brass was cleaning up.

They didn't even have to have the money to back the loan, all they had to do was sign off on somebody else's debt by loaning their credit rating, not their money, just their credit rating, and the money poured in to AIG. It's kind of like you cosigning for everybody on your block who wants to buy a new car. Odds are, somebody's not going to be able to pay, right? Well, what happens if suddenly more than half can't pay for their new wheels? Uh-oh!

That's what happened to AIG. The credit default swap was a complicated but brilliant financial scheme that left all of us holding the bag.

▧ Revolving Doors, All Over Again

The regulations could have been better, but the real sellouts were some regulators themselves.

Because the fact of the matter is that the regulations that were still in place were all but disregarded by some regulators who didn't want to offend their prospective employers. They wanted jobs. Financial writers like Robert Lenzner, national editor for *Forbes*, and CNN's financial guru Ali Velshi say the damage could have been diminished if more regulators had done their jobs more thoroughly.

> When people have superficial intentions, you wonder how long they will last in that position.

> Should be law that Regulators cannot work for Business they regulate for at least 10 years. Include Lobbying.

> I think many aspects of the system are flawed—corrupt even—but we should remember the honest members of society too.

> Its all about the Benjamins. Morality deceived them, and they deceived us.

Critics say we allowed the regulators to have a revolving door going from business to government and back again.

The revolving door extended into the Securities and Exchange Commission, the SEC, the agency that's supposed to serve as our watchdogs on Wall Street. They are the guys who are supposed to make sure the banks and investment firms follow the rules.

Some weren't making them follow the rules. Instead of making decisions for the good of all of us, were they making decisions based on what their next job was going to be?

Here's what Bill Black, a former federal regulator who's now a professor at the University of Missouri–Kansas City, told *Newsweek*: "The pay can be very bad, but it's not simply that the pay is low. The agency regulating the savings and loans was not permitted to pay as much as the U.S. Office of Personnel Management pays. So, in terms of the initial selection, the better people will go to the other agencies.

At the SEC, leading up to WorldCom and Enron, the turnover also became obscene. The average lawyer at the SEC stayed barely over two years, and your first year, you're kind of useless."

The takeaway is this: Even after lawmakers got rid of some of the regulations, there were still enough rules left on the books that should have been enforced. You ask why didn't enough regulators say, "Wait a minute, wait a minute, wait a minute. What's going on here?" Fact is, many did not!

What Madoff Made Off With

Then there's Bernie Madoff. The guy ran a multibillion-dollar Ponzi scheme right under the noses of the SEC. People literally called the regulators and said, "There's something funny going on here." There is actually one guy who'd even looked at Bernie Madoff's books and said, "This doesn't add up. You guys should take a look at this."

And experts say that many at the SEC just completely turned a blind eye to it. And not just once or twice. It turned out they had been getting complaints about Madoff since 1999 and, basically, ignoring them. Well, of course! Bernie was the former head of NASDAQ. He palled around with some of the top SEC regulators. And one of Madoff's former secretaries said some of the young SEC staffers who visited his headquarters often asked about job openings.

You and I could not believe what we were hearing, so I called Ali Velshi—I referred to him as a financial guru earlier, but his official title is CNN's chief business correspondent. I called him to ask him about the financial collapse and the role of regulators. Ali had just penned a book about the meltdown called *Gimme My Money Back.*

"We were paying them to be our watchdogs," I said. "Why didn't they act like watchdogs?"

"Pure and simple," Ali said. "Because they wanted better jobs."

They didn't want to be regulators. Regulator is the job that you have now. The job that a regulator wants later on is vice president for Morgan Stanley, or vice president for AIG. Or vice president for any of these giant Wall Street firms.

Now, do you think a giant Wall Street firm is going to hire somebody who made them jump through hoops and insisted they follow every little regulation? Of course not.

■ The Perfect Financial Storm

In the end, it became the perfect storm.

At the outset, when the crisis hit, I think it was just absolute confusion. Back in September and October of 2008, people were completely dumbfounded and had no idea what was going on.

The executives of these companies—most if not all of them— were convinced they'd be able to muscle their way out of this, just like they had in the past. They figured they would take out loans to cover their losses, then work to pay them off over time. That's the way it works, right? That's the way it always works.

But not this time. The thing that devastated the economy was that, this time, there were no loans. The system locked up.

Our financial system is very much like our circulatory system in our bodies. In other words, nothing works unless blood is flowing.

To stretch the analogy, Lehman Brothers would be the heart and AIG the brain, and Morgan Stanley—let's make them the liver.

Well, they always figured that the liver could just go to the heart and say, "Pump a little more blood this way, please." Or the brain could go to the heart and say, "I need another loan, give me another little bit of blood over here." So the heart would take a little extra from the liver and shift it over to the brain, or vice versa.

And that's always the way they had done it. They had been able to get themselves out of every hole by moving some from here to over there and back again. It was a circulatory gamble.

What happened during that particular time in our financial history was that the flow stopped. There was no blood circulating. Period. So there wasn't enough blood going around for the heart or the liver or the brain. When the CEO for the brain went in and said, "Hey, just give a little more blood over here and I'll be okay; just a little to get me through the next year," there was none.

The answer was: "Sorry. There's no blood."

Neither was there for the heart. Neither was there for the liver. But none of them knew that before because they were all working independently of everybody else. Now what happened was, we had a complete collapse, a complete shutdown of the system. It was on the brink of death. And if they didn't get the blood flowing again, if they didn't get the money flowing, the whole system would die.

The economy needed a transfusion. And the only way to get it was by having the Federal Reserve come in and essentially create money and pump it into the circulatory system, into the body of our financial system, to save it. We had to give these guys, essentially, what they didn't deserve, or we would all die.

The general public certainly didn't understand that, and asked, "Why should I pay?"

bull shit!!!!!!!!!

yes, I do think it would have happened.

Geithner used fears of high unemployment to justify the WS bailout b/c the gov't doesn't understand the financial sector.

yes; I firmly believe that if Grampy McCain would
have become POTUS, we would be in a worldwide
depression.

And now, as I have learned from reading the book *Too Big to Fail*
by Andrew Sorkin and interviewing him, even the guys who ran those
companies didn't know that. I mean, they went in screaming and yelling, "Come on, let's get the hell out of this."

As Sorkin explained on my show, these guys at the top were caught
by surprise as much as we were. And when it all exploded, they just
couldn't believe it was happening—not to them.

"You know," he said, "the book is called *Too Big to Fail* and people
talk about that phrase in the context of institutions. But I actually
think about it in the context of these people who think that they are
too big to fail. And there's an element of hubris and greed and power
that I think sort of runs throughout the narrative."

"Was it the schemes," I asked, "like the default swaps? Or was it
the fact the regulations had been gotten rid of? Or, in the end, was it
the fact that the regulators were asleep? Of those three things that
come to my mind . . ."

I was a little surprised by his answer.

"I actually don't think it's necessarily about fancy financial products or financial engineering," he said. "It's about debt. We loaded this
country up with debt. People took on too much debt. Companies took
on too much debt. Banks lent money they didn't have. And funda-
mentally, that was our basic problem."

Flatlining

What happened afterward was that the government did have to come
in and do this transfusion, as I call it.

I mean, again, think of it as a guy who's been in this terrible accident. His heart has stopped. There's no blood flowing. He's basically flatlining. That's what the paramedics used to call it as I was covering stories out of Miami. There's no pulse. This guy is gone.

But they were going to keep him alive just so they can get him to the hospital. They were going to put him on a ventilator. They were going to zap him with the defibrillator, to get his heart going. And they were going to start pumping in blood on an IV to keep him alive, until he got going on his own again.

That's what was happening with our economy back then. The economy was flatlining, and the government had to jump in—stat!—and give it a jolt to get its heart pumping, and then follow it up with a massive transfusion to offset all the blood it had lost in "toxic assets."

At that point, it was totally artificial. They were just trying to keep it alive. And if they didn't get money within a certain time to come back into the system, the whole thing would go out.

While the country was still struggling to understand the economic collapse, I took my show on the road to Georgia State University, where I spoke with the director of its Economic Forecasting Center, Rajeev Dhawan. He's an incredibly smart guy, who knows how to cut through the chaff and get down to plain language. He said, yeah, deregulation was partly to blame. So were the regulators. And so were all of us who enjoyed the easy credit and spent beyond our means.

For the answer to how to rescue the banking system, he reminded us of how Jimmy Stewart pulled his bank back from the brink in *It's a Wonderful Life*. When the bank was threatened with collapse, he took his honeymoon money and pumped it in, to keep the money flowing. Essentially, he gave it a transfusion of his own cash—some stimulus money.

That's what this professor said we needed to do as a nation. He was arguing that we did need to put money back into the system to keep it from collapsing.

I know some people who like to say that it was a global problem, so pumping our money in is just putting good money after bad. Well, it's a global problem because the rest of the world trusted us and bought into what we were doing. When we started creating default swaps and created this bizarre scheme at AIG and started moving money around, well, people thought it was coming from U.S. banks that had a AA or AAA rating, so it had to be okay.

So the Bank of England and the Bank of Ireland and all the banks around the world say, "Well, look, it's got a AAA rating. If Moody's says it's got a AAA rating, then obviously we must trust it."

So then the rest of the world started doing the very same thing we were doing. That's why, when we fell, the whole world fell. That's why there seemed to be a global collapse going on, not just an American one.

And that's why guys like Professor Dhawan argue you have to put the money back into that system that's broken and you have to do it right now or else the global repercussions will come back and kick us in the butt.

▓ Pump It Up!

That's what they think when it comes to the White House, too.

As the president was tussling with the meltdown, I spoke with Jared Bernstein, President Obama's chief economic policy advisor, at least every couple of weeks.

The White House is convinced that the $787 billion stimulus package that the Obama administration passed in early 2009 is going to, or has already, filtered enough money into the system to get us by for the short term. They know people are still worried about jobs, but the first thing they felt they had to do was shore up the economy so that there would be jobs in the long term.

Near the end of 2009, Bernstein told me he was convinced they were making inroads on credit and that money was starting to flow again in the system—that the circulatory thing I mentioned earlier was starting to work again. They were dealing with housing. They were dealing with the bank structure. And they were dealing with credit.

But looking at the numbers, the economic statistics out there, the economy was still incredibly weak. People were worried about the potential for double-digit unemployment; retailers were seeing people return to the stores for the holiday season, but they were spending less than in previous years; and houses were beginning to sell, but the foreclosure rate was still rising.

The folks across America didn't have to read the *Wall Street Journal* to know those things. Everybody knew somebody who'd been laid off—probably lots of them—and people were scared they'd be laid off themselves. They could see the foreclosure signs dotting their neighborhoods.

Yet they kept hearing about billions of dollars in bailout money flowing into these Wall Street firms and some Detroit automakers.

Finally, by April of this year we began to see signs that we were coming out of the recession. The Dow hit eleven thousand and the *Wall Street Journal* wrote a front-page story explaining how shoppers were turning up in surprising force at U.S. stores, auto dealerships, and restaurants, adding to the growing sense that the recovery could prove faster than anticipated. Finally, some good news.

But maybe the best news of all was that some bailout recipients were beginning to pay back our government money with interest.

Bailout Fatigue

But as the process of legislating trudged on, and as the first bailout packages were announced, I started reading your angry responses on

Twitter, MySpace, and Facebook saying, "Well, hold on a minute. Why should we as a people come up with our money to save these people who have screwed up everything that they have? They don't deserve this."

That's when I started using the term "bailout fatigue" to describe what I was seeing. People were angry about what had gone on. And people are still angry. They may not recognize it as being part of the same thing, but these folks who are out there yelling at the town halls and the tea parties, that is really a manifestation of that same anger.

It's interesting that it's all turned against Barack Obama. But hey, lonely is the head that wears the crown; nobody said it was going to be easy, Mr. President. The whole idea for the resuscitation plan, as I call it, or the transfusion plan, came from George Bush. It was President Bush who said our financial system is on the verge of collapse. Those are his words, not Barack Obama's words. But guess what? Obama signed on to it, so as many of his critics say, he now owns it.

Critics of President Obama also point to his choice of staff. The first thing he did was to hire Timothy Geithner and Larry Summers. Now, there are two arguments to this debate. On the one hand, yeah, if you want to know how to fix something that's broken, you better talk to people who have been inside that system. But the other argument is, why in the hell would you recruit from the same screwed-up system to fix the screwed-up system?

When I invited the documentary filmmaker Michael Moore on my show, right after he had come out with the movie *Capitalism: A Love Story*, he had a slightly different view of the situation.

"I wouldn't want the job," he said, "but he's brought in Mr. Geithner and Mr. Summers and Mr. Rubin, three of the architects of this mess. And it's kind of like how the big banks, they actually hire bank robbers to advise them on how to prevent bank robberies. So maybe President Obama has brought these three in to advise them on how to fix the mess they helped to create."

▨ Moving Forward

Here's what many experts say: We used to enforce the separation of the commercial banks and investment banks, which used to prevent us from falling into exactly the kind of crisis we suddenly found ourselves in. They say there's a reason savings and loans were set up differently from commercial banks. And they say there's a reason the investment banks were supposed to keep a certain amount of money in reserve, on hand in case of an emergency.

Many of the economists I interview now agree that if we don't somehow establish some of those safeguards again, we're just going to fall into the very same trap.

If you listen to this president's words, he's saying he's going to punish the people on Wall Street. And that he's going to create rules so they can't continue to do this again. Critics say he hasn't done enough, and there is plenty of evidence they are right. And then there are those who argue he should leave it alone and it will fix itself.

But experts I've interviewed say it seems painfully obvious that when we remove too many regulations and let Wall Street do what it wants, we all pay!

We're still paying for it. We're still suffering. Yet some people are arguing that it's wrong to put government back in the game as a check and balance.

That's when most of you scream, "What?!"

We've got a nightmare that we're trying to get out of and there are some people out there who are essentially trying to keep it going by saying, "No, no, let's continue that way. Let's continue what we were doing. Don't blame the rich Wall Street guys. They didn't do anything wrong."

Sarah Palin says cut taxes, cut payroll taxes, and slay the death taxes once and for all and you'll see the economy roar back to life. But critics ask, why would we do more of what got us in a giant hole? They say when you're in a hole, quit digging. Oh, and of course Palin continues to call Obama's policies socialist.

I asked Michael Moore about it when he was on my show, about the president being called a socialist.

"The only socialism I've seen in the last year is the welfare payments that we've made to Wall Street bailing them out," Moore said. "It's just so funny how up is down all of a sudden. . . . Yes, unfortunately, the people who call themselves capitalists got rid of capitalism." Moore was, as mentioned, pitching a movie about just that, capitalism.

Bad for Business

As Americans we defend capitalism. We say it's good. Big business is good. And that part of it is right. But totally unrestrained, big business is not good. Hell, totally unrestrained anything is not good!

At the end of the day, whether it's business, journalism, or parenting, you have to be able to look at yourself in the mirror.

I keep going back to my dad. My dad always taught me: "When you cheat, you cheat everybody. Most of all, you cheat yourself."

I don't care what the laws say, because there's something even more important than laws. For those of us who believe in God, there is that. Then there's also living with yourself. If at the end of the day you know that what you did is hurting people, then it doesn't matter if it's legal—it was wrong. I don't care how often you go to church. I don't care how much money you give to your church. The bottom line is: You're hurting the system.

There's no such thing as a utopia and that's why as Americans we need to regularly self-adjust.

We've become enamored with being rich. We've become enamored with business. We've become enamored with money. And now, some are arguing, in the process we may have forgotten what's good for America. We seem to need some measure of self-control:

laissez faire is utopia and socialism is extreme.
Happy medium is best.

if big business "fixed" everything—we wouldn't be in the mess were in.

I tell them "sorry you were never taught about the Golden Rule."

CHAPTER 6

You're Sick of Wars

"The enemy of my enemy is my friend."

How odd that that oft-quoted proverb originates among Arabs.

How ironic that it wasn't heeded when it came to Saddam Hussein and Osama bin Laden. When we attacked Saddam Hussein's country, we were attacking the enemy of our enemy (bin Laden).

First, let's start with a refresher: Were there weapons of mass destruction in Iraq? *No*, check!

Was Saddam Hussein involved in the planning or execution of the 9/11 attacks? *No*, check!

Was Saddam Hussein involved in the operation of al-Qaeda? *No*, check!

Did Saddam Hussein hate bin Laden? According to news reports, *Yes!*

Did bin Laden hate Saddam Hussein? According to news reports, *Yes!*

Can I make it any clearer? *Okay*, I will.

According to an article in the *Guardian* in 2003, Osama bin Laden twice suggested or ordered the assassination of Saddam Hussein. And he begrudgingly went along with defending Iraqis, but always let it be known he hated Saddam, "the evil socialist." So it's pretty clear, bin Laden was not a Saddam fan.

How about Saddam's feelings for bin Laden? Listen to this: According to a *60 Minutes* report by correspondent Scott Pelley in 2008, Saddam Hussein "didn't want to associate" with bin Laden. Moreover, Saddam viewed bin Laden "as a threat to him and his regime." We at CNN have reported on these developments extensively, though many of you say not enough:

> that was largely ignored. Everyone knew it. We
> invaded Iraq for the oil and bases.

> because the administration lied and the media went
> right along with the whole charade.

Then there are those of you who say so what, even without the original reason given for war, taking out Saddam was worth it:

> why defend him? he is a killer, ANY way you look at.

> Lets see—try to assassinate a POTUS, Paid families
> for suicide bombing in Israel, used Germ warfare.

The U.S. attack on Afghanistan, considering the circumstances at the time it was launched, seemed to almost all Americans to be the right war for the right reason. It seemed inevitable that the country from where Osama bin Laden planned and ordered the worst attacks on the U.S. since Pearl Harbor would bear the brunt of the United States' military vengeance. But it could have been over quickly!

Here's what is criticized. The most infamous name in international terrorism besides bin Laden belonged to Ayman al-Zawahiri. The Egyptian doctor founded the Muslim Brotherhood, which is in many ways the forerunner of al-Qaeda. There is no question al-Zawahiri was involved in the planning and execution of 9/11. Mullah Omar was the leader of the Taliban, who had welcomed, hosted, and embraced bin Laden and all that he represented in Afghanistan, including the 9/11 attacks on the United States. And then there's bin Laden himself. We know what he represents. The trio was targeted, and each was publicly singled out as the face or faces of the attacks against America. Taking them on, taking them out, and/or bringing them to justice was as much a military necessity as it was an American moral necessity.

Yet, it wasn't accomplished. All three, as of the writing of this book, are still alive and reportedly well enough to carry on a propaganda campaign against the West with taped messages containing threats, and possibly orders that are heard around the world. We failed!

Military commanders with whom I have spoken say it needed to be done with boots on the ground in Afghanistan, not half-assedly.

Many of you ask, why did we do it half-assedly? According to some military commanders I queried, Vice President Dick Cheney and Secretary Rumsfeld convinced President Bush to not put more boots on the ground. In fact, they had another target in mind. That's according to a series of interviews I have done with commanders who were on the ground in Afghanistan.

Republican senator Lindsey Graham of South Carolina says today of how we should proceed in that part of the world moving forward; "We shouldn't Rumsfeld it!"

▉ Sorry, Richard, Wrong Answer!

And then there's Richard Clarke. He says he tried to convince high-ranking members of the Bush administration even prior to 9/11 that al-Qaeda and bin Laden, and al-Zawahiri, should be targeted. Clarke knew terrorism as well as anyone. He worked on it while serving four U.S. presidents. He helped shape U.S. policy on terrorism under President Reagan and the first President Bush. He was held over by President Clinton to be his terrorism czar, then held over again by the second President Bush. But when he first approached administration insiders about reviewing and possibly renewing Clinton administration policies on al-Qaeda and bin Laden, he says he was told that President Clinton was "obsessed with bin Laden." Clarke says he couldn't even get a meeting with anybody in the administration to hear him out.

"We had a terrorist organization that was going after us! Al-Qaeda, that should have been the first item on the agenda. And it was pushed back and back and back for months.

"There's a lot of blame to go around, and I probably deserve some blame, too. But on January 24th, 2001, I wrote a memo to Condoleezza Rice asking for, urgently—underlined urgently—a Cabinet-level meeting to deal with the impending al-Qaeda attack. And that urgent memo wasn't acted on," Clarke told *60 Minutes.*

"I blame the entire Bush leadership for continuing to work on Cold War issues when they got back in power in 2001. It was as though they were preserved in amber from when they left office eight years earlier. They came back. They wanted to work on the same issues right away: Iraq, Star Wars. Not new issues, the new threats that had developed over the preceding eight years."

Then came 9/11, and Clarke finally got his meeting with the president.

"The president dragged me into a room with a couple of other people, shut the door, and said, 'I want you to find whether Iraq did this.' Now, he never said, 'Make it up.' But the entire conversation left me in absolutely no doubt that George Bush wanted me to come back with a report that said Iraq did this.

"I said, 'Mr. President. We've done this before. We have been looking at this. We looked at it with an open mind. There's no connection.'

"He came back at me and said, 'Iraq! Saddam! Find out if there's a connection.' And in a very intimidating way. I mean that we should come back with that answer. We wrote a report."

Clarke, who now writes extensively about counterterrorism, says he disagreed with what the administration wanted to do and said so in a report, but he doubts the president ever saw his report. Clarke gave this description in 2004 to *60 Minutes*:

"We got together all the FBI experts, all the CIA experts. We wrote the report. We sent the report out to CIA and said, 'Will you sign this report?' They all cleared the report. And we sent it up to the president and it got bounced by the National Security Advisor or Deputy. It got bounced and sent back saying, 'Wrong answer. . . . Do it again.'"

Clarke has since become a frequent guest on my afternoon show. He told me point-blank that he is convinced Vice President Dick Cheney was pulling the strings, and that he didn't believe it was President Bush's decision to spin the Iraqi threat.

"I have no idea, to this day, if the president saw it, because after we did it again, it came to the same conclusion. And frankly, I don't think the people around the president show him memos like that. I don't think he sees memos that he doesn't—wouldn't like the answer."

The early years of the Iraq War have been called many things, but one word few Americans would use to describe that period is a "strategic success." Despite losing more than forty-three hundred of our bravest and most duty-bound soldiers, Iraq is still an unsettled issue. The country is still dangerous, while bin Laden, al-Zawahiri, and Omar roam free.

Yes, there have been some successes. Relentless bombings threatened to derail recent elections, but their election with a 55 to 60 percent turnout proved impressive. That's comparable to U.S. turnout, which was 56.8 percent in 2008.

Still, many, many of you seem convinced, as you tell me frequently, that the billions spent every month fighting in both Iraq and Afghanistan have helped bankrupt our nation. Many of you also say that the use of torture and the seeming lack of cultural understanding has rekindled and solidified lingering resentments, and turned a once sympathetic world against us. Your thoughts:

> no, we lost valuable lives for a country that will only
> fall back into chaos.

> It was NOT worth it . . . billions wasted, thousands of
> lives lost, and we are deeper in debt.

Vice President Dick Cheney remained steadfast in his disagreement with his detractors and with critics of the Iraq War. He told ABC News in 2008 that Iraq was the right decision despite what we got wrong about WMD and Saddam's ties or lack thereof to al-Qaeda and 9/11.

"I think we made the right decision in spite of the fact that the original [intelligence estimate] was off in some of its major judgments," Cheney said.

"Saddam Hussein still had the capability to produce weapons of mass destruction. He had the technology [and] he had the people . . . [He] had every intention of resuming production once the international sanctions were lifted. This was a bad actor."

Still, the majority of you tell me you're angry about how the war has turned out. And CNN polls have shown support for the war in Iraq has dwindled steadily.

But for some it's hard to express. Because we so admire and respect our troops, many of us find it difficult to criticize what some call the foolhardy political decisions that led to their deaths, disfigurements, and nightmares, while bin Laden was allowed to get away.

Yes, I said and reported on my show, "*Allowed* to get away."

Armageddon

Pretty close to a month after I got to MSNBC, 9/11 happened.

I was sitting in the makeup room getting ready to go on the air when I looked up at a TV in the corner and saw this plane heading into the World Trade Center.

I immediately ran into the head of MSNBC's office and said, "Get me there. I want to cover this story."

MSNBC's offices were in New Jersey at that time. So I jumped on a PATH train that goes under the Hudson River from Hoboken to downtown Manhattan. It turned out to be the very last one going in before they shut them down to stop people from heading into what would become a disaster zone.

As soon as I got across, I grabbed a cab and raced to the Twin Towers. It was surreal.

I remember that as we got out of the cab, I turned to face the Trade Center and we watched as the second tower started crashing to the ground. I couldn't believe what I was seeing. It was the moment that will forever be frozen in time.

All of a sudden, a giant cloud of smoke started rushing toward us. As the debris hit the ground it formed a cloud that went from the ground up, filling the space between buildings and racing toward us. People were running and screaming. Everyone was running toward me, away from the collapse, as we were headed in the opposite direction, toward the Trade Center.

I never made it. I realized the dust cloud was too stifling, too enormous to see through, so I ducked into a garage. I remember being welcomed into the garage by a mechanic, a Ukrainian, and he was taking people in who were seeking shelter. His lined face was that of a hardworking immigrant, and his expression seemed to say, "Not here, not in America too," as if he'd experienced this type of thing before.

As the smoke cleared, I stepped out again and started walking into the debris. I felt so alone. There were police and firefighters everywhere, but they seemed as dazed and confused as all others. Everything was still.

Fires were burning. Bodies lay amid fallen parts of buildings. It's as if civilization had stopped and everything was just left as it was when the buildings came crashing down. So eerie.

My mouth felt like I had eaten cotton mixed with engine fluid. The smoke was filling my lungs and my face and clothing were dust white. I was parched. So I walked into what was left of a McDonald's. It was still; obviously abandoned in a hurry, empty. Unsold French fries and Big Macs were being warmed by a heat lamp, and two shakes sat on the counter. I felt guilty taking one of them without paying, and actually wondered if anyone would care. Then I went outside, sat on the sidewalk alone, amid this Armageddon, called my mother, then my wife, described the scene and cried.

As we made our way closer still to the actual downed Twin Towers, police officers were screaming, "Get away! Get away! There might be a bomb that's going to go off." The police officers who were there for some reason were convinced that it wasn't just the planes that had exploded. They seemed to think and were telling one another, and me and anyone who would listen, that there were bombs in the area. That was disproven later, but to this day people quote Rick Sanchez reports because I mentioned what those police officers had told me.

We finally found the NBC Live truck that had made its way near ground zero. I could hear Brian Williams in my ear, saying, "Let's go to Rick Sanchez, who's standing by, right off of Canal Street, right near the scene of the attack. Rick, what do you have?"

I don't know what happened. I don't know if I was still intimidated because I was less than a month into my first network job, or I was just in shock over what I had just seen. But I could barely get my mouth to work. I sounded dazed and robotic as I said, "We are standing here on the corner near Canal Street, where I'm seeing a lot of people. They've been moving in directions." Williams must have thought, "What's wrong with this guy?"

You can probably still find it on the Internet. It's easily one of the worst news reports I've ever filed. It almost seemed like I was disoriented and didn't know what I was doing. To be fair, to be honest, I had just witnessed one of the most brazen, bizarre, deadly acts I've ever seen in my life, and I was shaken. We all were. But I was supposed to keep my head. I sucked. I'm embarrassed to this day to have to say it, but it's the truth.

As would become clear over the hours and days that followed, our nation was under attack for the first time since Pearl Harbor. Thousands of innocent people had been killed in the name of a jihad by a madman many Americans had never heard of, but who, in a matter of minutes, changed our lives forever.

■ Al-Qaeda and Afghanistan

Soon enough, we would all know the name of Osama bin Laden. And within a matter of days we were piecing together the details of the attack.

U.S. intelligence officials identified the nineteen hijackers, and we learned how they had trained for the mission right under our very noses. We learned how they made the preparations, and how, on that fateful morning, they had pulled out box cutters, taken control of the planes, and flown them and their horrified passengers into their targets.

This was the first almost all of us had ever heard of bin Laden, or al-Qaeda. But now we knew them, and knew what they had done. And we wanted revenge.

So, as we learned that they had been aided by the Taliban, and that bin Laden was believed to be in Afghanistan, we were more than willing to attack.

And there was evidence that most of the world supported us.

The day after the Twin Towers collapsed, the world's sentiment was summed up by the Parisian newspaper *Le Monde*, with the headline: "Today, we are all American." I mean, heck, when you've got the Frenchies on your side, you must be getting universal support, right? And it really wasn't just them. Moderate Arabs in Asia and Africa seemed to feel our pain, and shared our outrage.

So when we went into Afghanistan with what appeared to be a clear mission, Americans cheered and the rest of the world went along.

U.S. troops quickly proved that America was ready, able—and angry. U.S. troops, aided by Afghan alliances, overwhelmed the Taliban defenders. They swept across the Afghan terrain in relentless pursuit of our target. All of America seemed united behind the war effort and punishing the people who attacked so many of our innocents.

The mission seemed to be going as planned. Americans were feeling vindicated. The president's poll numbers were through the roof. All was good with the state of war, as I covered it for hours on end during the day-side hours on MSNBC—every strategy, every corridor in every province, names and terms you and I were learning together, like the Northern Alliance and Afghan warlords. There were the Pashtuns, who made up about 40 percent of the country; the Tajiks, who made up about 30 percent; and then there were the Uzbeks and Hazaras, who made up much of the rest. What's a warlord? What's the difference between an Uzbek and a Pashtun? You can only imagine what our soldiers were going through trying to figure it all out while in combat. But figure it out they did.

Because less than three months after 9/11, Osama bin Laden was cornered and, military commanders tell me, we "let him get away."

Pay close attention to that sentence: He didn't escape. According to several extensive interviews I've conducted with military commanders on the ground, we let him get away.

Did We Let Him Get Away?

Here's how Republican senator John McCain answered Tim Russert in 2008 on the question of getting bin Laden: "I wouldn't have passed up on some of the opportunities we passed up, such as Tora Bora."

I wanted to know more about what McCain and others who've made this charge about Tora Bora really meant. Cheney, Rumsfeld, and Tommy Franks all refute McCain's "passed up opportunity" claim. They have said repeatedly they never really knew bin Laden's location.

Recently released reports and accounts from eyewitnesses on the battlefield suggest that by the second week of December, the marines and elite army and CIA Special Forces teams had Osama bin Laden trapped like a scared rabbit in the caves in Tora Bora. The head of the CIA paramilitary team there, Gary Berntsen, says he asked for an additional eight hundred U.S. Army Rangers so he could go and get him. Eight hundred men that he was convinced would have gotten the job done. Bin Laden was trapped.

Request denied. No reason given.

That's the account of both Commander Berntsen and Afghanistan CIA Chief Hank Crumpton, who led the CIA's Afghan campaign in 2001. I called Crumpton for his account and I invited Berntsen on *Rick's List* to learn his version of events.

Berntsen said the decision had to have come from the highest levels in the chain of command—at the White House—and the reason was clear:

"It was a political decision," he said.

He explained that he called in his request to CENTCOM, U.S.

Central Command, the military authority in charge of the Afghan operation, headed at the time by General Tommy Franks. From there, Berntsen said, it went straight upstairs.

"What would occur is Hank Crumpton [head of the CIA's Counterterrorism Center's Special Operations unit], [CIA Director] George Tenet, uh, the Vice-President, the President, the Secretary of Defense would have a meeting at the White House and the decision was made there to use the Pakistani Frontier Force instead of using the eight hundred Rangers that I had requested," said Berntsen.

A little later in the interview, I pressed the issue.

"But just to be clear," I said, "so we don't think it's like some underling somewhere in some office made this decision . . ."

"No," he said, "it was no underling, it was no underling. This was briefed at the highest level in the White House. And Mr. Crumpton has been on television . . . explaining what my request was."

Berntsen's account is in fact corroborated by Hank Crumpton, who says he briefed Bush, as well as Vice President Dick Cheney and General Franks, about the need to go after bin Laden in Tora Bora at the time.

Gary C. Schroen, the CIA field officer in charge of the initial CIA operation in Afghanistan after 9/11, also corroborates Berntsen's account. Schroen is the author of *First In: An Insider's Account of How the CIA Spearheaded the War on Terror in Afghanistan*.

Here's his exchange with Tim Russert in late 2004:

TIM RUSSERT: In October 2004, General Tommy Franks offered this observation: "We don't know to this day whether Mr. bin Laden was at Tora Bora in December 2001. Mr. bin Laden was never within our grasp." You just disagree with that?

GARY C. SCHROEN: I absolutely do, yes.

RUSSERT: And President Bush and Vice President Cheney all quoted General Franks saying. "We don't know if bin Laden was at Tora Bora." You have no doubt?

SCHROEN: I have no doubt that he was there.

Three accounts by three men all seeming to equal the same thing. Former defense secretary Donald Rumsfeld and former Iraq commander Tommy Franks have continued to insist all along that they didn't know of any evidence that bin Laden was actually in Tora Bora at the time.

I wanted to know more about this back-and-forth, so I asked Berntsen for more details. I figured he was there, so he's the one to ask for specifics.

For example, is it possible that Franks and Rumsfeld really didn't know specifically where bin Laden was? Tora Bora was, after all, a huge area, right?

Berntsen was adamant. "Not true," he said. He told me he had pinpointed exactly where bin Laden was hiding.

"Pinpointed exactly?" I thought. No kidding. I wanted more information, like how?

"We had human sources who actually delivered food and water to him," he said. "At one point, we followed him with a fifteen-thousand-pound device, a Blue 82, to actually kill him. We killed a lot of his folks with the device. We were listening to him on the phone because all of his sophisticated como went down. They were using hunting radios. At one point we had one of them and we were listening. There were other ways that we knew as well, believe me. We knew he was there. . . ."

A Senate report issued last December agreed. It said a review of unclassified government records and interviews with participants "removes any lingering doubts and makes it clear that Osama bin Laden was within our grasp at Tora Bora."

When you read the Senate report you can't help but ask, what the hell was the top brass thinking? They had guys on the ground, listening in on bin Laden and ready to go grab him by the beard and drag him out, and they decided that they didn't want to get him—why??

Instead, the United States let him slip out the back door and mosey off into Pakistan.

"The vast array of American military power, from sniper teams to the most mobile divisions of the Marine Corps and the Army, was kept on the sidelines," the report said. So, bin Laden "walked unmolested out of Tora Bora and disappeared into Pakistan's unregulated tribal area."

Why would we let him get away?

Was it because the Afghan war was not a priority? Was it that the real war that Cheney wanted to fight, as Clarke suggests, was in Iraq?

So you ask, how is it possible that the war that made the most sense to most Americans was actually not as important?

Look at what happened next.

Look at the three really bad guys who attacked us—al-Zawahiri, bin Laden, and Omar, who protected them. They are the ones grabbing the headlines, the ones we supposedly went into Afghanistan to get. Okay. So after bin Laden escapes from the cave where Delta Force commanders and CIA guys were convinced they had him cornered, he waltzes away and is never seen again, except on tape.

Why weren't they good targets? Isn't bin Laden a good target? How about al-Zawahiri or Mullah Omar? Aren't those pretty good targets on the heels of 9/11?

But the decision was made to send our troops to Iraq at the now apparent expense of finishing the job in Afghanistan.

The War is a disgrace, the lives. We could have
used the $ to insure the American people. This war
has brought America to its knees.

Bush II wanted vengeance 4 dad.

You tell me, both on the right and left, that you began to sour on
the wars. You began to take your frustration out on George W. Bush,
who in turn took out his apparent frustration on Rumsfeld by essentially firing him after defending him for months prior.

Total waste of taxpayers' money.

bin Laden is laughing his ass off. We are fools.

Then came the Senate Foreign Relations Committee's report,
which essentially agreed with many of your comments.

It stated: "Removing the al-Qaida leader from the battlefield eight
years ago would not have eliminated the worldwide extremist threat,"
the Senate report now says. "But the decisions that opened the door
for his escape to Pakistan allowed bin Laden to emerge as a potent
symbolic figure who continues to attract a steady flow of money and
inspire fanatics worldwide. The failure to finish the job represents a
lost opportunity that forever altered the course of the conflict in Afghanistan and the future of international terrorism."

The report seems to be saying that bin Laden was allowed to slip
out the back door.

Think about it. If we had taken out Osama bin Laden right then
and there, might it all have been over? There certainly would have
been articles in newspapers that said, "We got him. Osama bin Laden
is dead." Americans would have cheered and finally gone on with their

lives. Would it have ended the national need for retribution, for any or all of the wars? We will never know, will we?

■ Reverse Dominoes

Recent election results in Iraq demonstrate an impressive turnout and an obvious hunger by Iraqis to establish a democracy. And that is exactly what architects of the Iraq War envisioned.

But has it been worth it? And was it the real aim?

Here are the arguments we've been given for invading Iraq: There are really three arguments, beginning with the two that have been universally refuted. There was no tie to al-Qaeda. And there were no weapons of mass destruction.

We know that. That's been proven again and again. Even President Bush has said so.

So, what's left? It's the Wolfowitz plan. I call it the Reverse Dominoes plan. When I interviewed Paul Wolfowitz, he was very resolute and honest about this. And I believe he was sincere.

Paul Wolfowitz told me, "If we are able to create democracy in Iraq, it would spread throughout the region, help democratize the region."

Remember Vietnam? The argument for us going to fight that war, the reason they said it was so vital to America, was that if the communists won in Vietnam, then the countries around it would start to fall to communism one after another, like dominoes, and communism would spread across the rest of the region.

This is the reverse dominoes theory. They believed that maybe if they could go in there and create a democracy in Iraq, then it would spread to the entire Middle East. Peace would spread throughout the region, oil would flow freely, and Israel would no longer be threatened. It was a well-intentioned strategy, but it didn't seem to work as planned.

The problem is, and most foreign-affairs experts now agree, you can't force a region to democratize, any more than you can expect them to "welcome you as liberators" after invading and occupying their country. Historians would point to the Moors, the Crusades, the Norman Conquest, the Hans, hell, even our own American Revolution would have sufficed!

The Wolfowitz plan outlined a democracy, and the jury is still out as to whether it will work when we pull our troops out of Iraq. The question underlined by his theory, though, is will it spread? Middle East experts say the answer so far is No, it has not!

But back then, Paul Wolfowitz convinced me and I'm sure many of my colleagues that it could. And he was one of the architects of the Iraq War, and served as deputy secretary of defense when the war began so he certainly had the gravitas to be taken seriously.

It's important to note that much of what Wolfowitz believed about Iraq was not something he came up with overnight. Five years earlier, he helped prepare and signed a document for the "Project for a New American Century," suggesting that Iraq be democratized by force. Many of his critics cite that as proof he intended to invade Iraq all along. But it also may show a consistency to his principles, regardless of his critics' attacks on his intentions.

Intentions aside, the reality of the Iraq War is it has been unkind to the Wolfowitz theory. Since we've been in Iraq, the Middle East has not democratized, and it has remained just as hostile.

So there you have the third reason, the third justification for war that Middle East experts say simply hasn't panned out.

So, what's left? Well, what you have left is regime change. And early supporters of the war cling to that argument like a life raft in a storm. "The world is a lot better off without Saddam Hussein and aren't you glad we got rid of him?"

Yes, most Americans are glad. But then they ask why we are still there if the regime has changed.

Brave soldiers and innocent civilians died when
there was no justifiable cause for war.

being a veteran, I really can't see the benefit of the
war in Iraq. We lost a lot of good people over there.

Here's what former Iraqi commander Ricardo Sanchez told me:
"It's a nightmare with no end in sight!" That's not what Rick Sanchez says, it's what Rick Sanchez says. General Ricardo (Rick) Sanchez told me, "Iraq was plagued from the outset by institutional and individual failures." He said we had lost "credibility within the country."

When I asked him how we get it back, he said there's only one way.

"A truth commission, I believe, is the only way to regain that."

CHAPTER 7

You're Sick of Religion Used as a Bludgeon

There's a holy war of sorts going on. Not just in Iraq or Afghanistan, but right here at home.

It's the one being waged by our own brand of religious zealots. It's a fight where some have purposely replaced the *D* in GOD with a *P*.

To be sure, there are ideological zealots who use mean-spirited tactics on both sides of the political divide. Certain WTO protestors are a good example. Their zealotry isn't based on religion, but as I pointed out recently on a long thread of tweets that got lots of attention on the blogs, "What else would you call anarchists who trash, pillage and throw Molotov cocktails at any and all gatherings where world business leaders converge?" It's undeniable that their embrace of these tactics has set these protestors apart and gained them the label, among their critics, of "lefty loonies."

But there's also no denying that since the election of President Obama—as pointed out by experts who follow such trends—there has been a rise in hate from hateful ideologues who very often base their objections on, oddly enough, the Bible. It's what I've spent many a segment on *Rick's List* analyzing and will try to explain here.

We've seen instances where God's words are being mixed in with political or ideological opinions, and those who dare disagree with those opinions are attacked.

The mixing of political and religious ideology leads too many to believe that anyone who challenges them is a nonbeliever, and thereby also not a good or patriotic American.

I've reported on some of those who most ardently lead this battle and seem to want you to believe that the president is a Muslim. They not only insist on blurring the line that separates church and state, they've actually convinced themselves that there is no line, that our Founding Fathers never really wanted to separate church and state.

To defend the argument they say the phrase "separation of church and state" is not found in the Constitution. They're correct. But here's the problem with that argument. You know what else isn't in the Constitution? Let's see, the words "right to a fair trial" aren't there—should we get rid of that, too?

There is also nothing in the Constitution about "the right to vote" or "the right to a jury of your peers." You want to get rid of those? Fact is, separation of church and state *was* a guiding principle of the Founding Fathers. It was nailed down by President Thomas Jefferson in 1801 in a letter written to the Danbury Baptists in which he wrote about the need for a "wall of separation" between church and state. And it is part of the foundation of who we are as a country.

Take down that wall, and what would we be left with? Would we then have to use religion to vet our judges all the way up to the Supreme Court? Would we have to inject a particular ideology in our schools? Where would it stop?

> please tell me you are covering the Texas education board changing the curriculum and taking out Thomas Jefferson?
>
> sep of church and state was to keep state out of church, not other way around.

That should be frightening to people, especially to politicians who insist they want less government intrusion in our lives. In case they don't understand the danger of mixing government with religion, many would be happy to hold up an example: the Taliban in Afghanistan. Need I say more?

The current of reported incidents of religious radicalism seen across the nation today goes far beyond the political activism that the Moral Majority engaged in two decades ago. Today's extremism is showing itself in ugly ways. I did a segment on my show about a pastor who went so far as to suggest in his Sunday sermon at his church that it would be okay to kill the president, and that he prays for it himself.

The funny thing is, because I've aggressively reported on these incidents, some have accused me of being a nonbeliever. Far from it!

As Americans, and as Christians, if you happen to be one, an argument is and should be made for not letting fanatics use the Bible as a shield to do and say whatever they want—hate masked as religion is still hate.

It makes you angry when you see it, and you tell me about it. But many of you are even more tired of the people who are driving that fanaticism and who use it for their own ends. You're sick of the politicos, the commentators, and the preachers who use religion to control others and attack anyone who's different.

Finding God

As Americans we believe that religion is a personal thing and none of anyone else's business. But in order to get to the heart of what I'm trying to say in this chapter, I'd like to tell you a story about my own spirituality, my own personal connection to God and why I believe. It was St. Peter who led me to God; actually, two St. Peters.

I'll explain.

When I graduated from college, I landed a fantastic job at a TV station in Miami. I was pinching myself. Talk about "hometown kid does good!" Here I was, fresh out of school, working at one of the stations I had grown up watching—and one where my mom and dad could see me every night. It was 1983 and I signed a contract for $17,000 a year, which seemed like so much money I'd need a wheelbarrow to carry it home every week.

Within a year I had won an Emmy award for a documentary on Cuba. Within two years, I was anchoring the weekend news. I was twenty-two years old, and I was already reporting and anchoring.

So I was moving fast—maybe too fast.

Everybody seemed to know who I was, especially in the heavily Hispanic enclave where I was seen as the kid who was breaking through in "American TV." Everywhere I went, people said hello. They wanted to shake my hand. They wanted my autograph. It was heady stuff—especially for a stupid kid fresh out of college who never really had the preparation to handle this kind of attention.

Miami was in its heyday. There was all kinds of stuff going on. And I was getting famous right in the middle of the *Miami Vice* era. I could go to the bars, and I would see the guys who were shooting and acting in *Miami Vice*, and the actors would say, "Hey, Sanchez! Come on over. Let me buy you a drink."

They picked my brain for possible Miami crime story lines. Little did I know I was on my way toward becoming one of those story lines. It was all happening too fast. I was too young. I was too inexperienced. I was taking success for granted.

And then I met a guy named Alberto San Pedro. San Pedro, by the way, means St. Peter in Spanish. He was St. Peter number one.

We met at a club in Coconut Grove at a time when drinks flowed freely and so did the white powder that would become infamous during the heyday of the cocaine cowboys. He came up and said, "Rick

Sanchez, you make us all proud. My name is Alberto San Pedro, and I live in Hialeah. Let me buy you a drink."

So Alberto San Pedro came along at a time in my life when I was pretty damn immature. Here was this guy who was sucking up to me and who had a lot of money and power. He drove three or four different cars. He had bodyguards. And I thought it was kind of cool to hang out with him. I just thought he was being nice to me, inviting me to all these wonderful places. I was honored by it.

Little did I know that maybe I was serving his purpose. That maybe I was legitimizing him. As far as my social life was concerned, it was great. He took me to the hottest nightclubs, where I met some of the hottest and best-looking women in Miami—who I could not impress with my salary, but I didn't have to. Al San Pedro was there for that. He bought the drinks and the dinners and whatever else was needed to keep the parties going.

I also knew San Pedro's other thing was politics. And there wasn't a single politician in Miami he didn't seem to influence. That made him a double whammy for me. He was my social buddy and my best source for figuring out who was doing what. Who was on the take and who wasn't.

Alberto San Pedro was an old-fashioned influence peddler. Just like the old-world politicos in Chicago, New York, Boston, L.A., and elsewhere, he knew how the wheels turned and how to grease them. He traded favors among some of the most influential people around town. And in the months that I got to know him I began to understand how politics really works, which may be why to this day I have very little tolerance for elected officials. Why would a grown man or woman want a job as mayor or commissioner that pays less than $10,000 a year? San Pedro knew it was either ego or greed that drove most of them, and he could feed either.

Then the music stopped and the drink well ran dry. It turns out that while I was hanging on every word Alberto San Pedro had to say, the police were hanging on every word as well—except they were doing it through a wire they got his girlfriend to wear. Roxanna Greene was part of the San Pedro group that hit the clubs and the bars. She was tall, buxom, and exotically beautiful. Like most of us growing up in that generation, she could switch from English to Spanish and back again on a dime. I liked her and she liked me, but I knew she was off-limits. She seemed smart and trustworthy. Little did I or anyone else know she was also wearing a wire and was secretly recording every single conversation for the Miami Organized Crime Bureau. This went on for months. She also helped police place bugs in San Pedro's office, his phones, and his car.

I was a young, single twenty-something living in one of the coolest town-house communities in Miami. Miami Lakes was South Florida's first modern planned community. It's where Don Shula, Dan Marino, and most of the Miami Dolphins lived. And it's where I lived—right off of Kilmarnock Drive on a beautiful lake surrounded by European townhomes.

One morning, I got out of bed, fed my cat, Mr. Trotsky, took a jog around the park, and then sat down to watch the noon news on TV. No sooner had the up-tempo music started, announcing a news bulletin, than I realized my life was about to spin out of control. I sat there absolutely stunned and frozen as I watched my friend and source Alberto San Pedro, in handcuffs, being walked out of his house, where just the weekend prior I had stopped by to have a glass of scotch on my way home from work.

It was, to say the very least, as if someone had dumped a bucket of cold water on me. I heard the reporter saying, "Police say wiretaps from inside San Pedro's home reveal a host of associates—key figures in the South Florida scene from federal to state to local politicians and beyond."

I knew right then and there that I was about to be embroiled in one hell of a controversy, because I knew I had been recorded in countless conversations that might be difficult to explain.

It didn't matter that I hadn't committed or taken part in any crimes. What mattered was I was associating with a guy the media was portraying as the second coming of Al Capone. And at the time the parallel seemed to fit. It was an embarrassing association. And soon I found myself in a closed-door meeting in my boss's office with an entire newsroom trying to look through the glass.

News Director Dave Choate was a kindhearted, old-fashioned journalist who was the very reason I went to work at the Miami NBC affiliate. I could have worked at ABC or CBS, but Choate seemed like the man to work for, because he was genuine.

"I can't believe this is happening. You were on a path to become the biggest name in broadcast journalism in South Florida, the first Cuban-American anchor." Choate continued, "And I was going to be there with you, but now it's over. It's all gone," he said, with mist gathering around the bottom of his eyes.

"I didn't commit any crimes, I've done nothing illegal, why's it over?" I asked, now tearing up myself.

"Because this story is going to be in the news for a year if not longer, and every time it comes up you come up," he explained. "You're damaged, you're tainted, and I got to let you go."

A dagger through the heart would not have hurt so much. I was embroiled in a controversy that had no end in sight. This thing was going to drag on for who knew how long. It was going to be in the news every single day.

And my boss said: "You have to go on the air every day and do the news, and the lead story on every newscast is going to be Alberto San Pedro. It's impossible for you to do the news in a town where the news is someone who you were involved with."

I was guilty by association. But they were right. I was tainted. I had to leave town, maybe for good.

Unemployed, maybe unemployable, and unsure if somehow I'd be called as a witness and dragged into some kind of legal quagmire, I got into my Chevy Camaro and just drove. I was scared, scarred, and hurting something awful. I didn't even want to face my mom and dad. I felt I had let them down. I stopped in rest stops and slept in my car—in parks, on the side of roads.

Prosecutors were playing games with me, as they were with everyone else whose name had turned up on the wiretaps. They figured just in case we knew something, they'd scare it out of us. I wasn't associated in drug deals, or payoffs, or anything of the sort, but they didn't know that. And it didn't stop me from thinking I really did know something. I thought maybe I would end up in jail, or worse, San Pedro's connections would rub me out just like in the movies to make sure I didn't talk. My mind was playing tricks on me. I was caught up in something I really didn't even understand; something I hadn't thought of when I was partying and having fun with the high rollers. I was stupid! And now I would pay!

I contemplated suicide. It was such an unbelievable fall. And it was so public. It was *the* story in South Florida at the time. It was South Florida's version of the O. J. Simpson trial, and I was caught smack dab in the middle of it. Everyone seemed to be whispering my name, another reason I had to leave town.

It wasn't just me, of course. It was anybody who had crossed this guy's path. And because Alberto San Pedro was an influence peddler, he crossed paths with a lot of people. He made sure that if you were famous or influential in South Florida and he got a chance to meet you somewhere, he was going to buy you a drink and call you from time to time.

It turns out that most of the people he associated with didn't do anything wrong. But we all got dragged into it, celebrities, judges, the attorney general, senators, and the list goes on.

The real pain I felt was over my family and my name and my image. I couldn't look my dad in the eye because I knew I had just totally screwed everything up. I had been given this wonderful opportunity, and I totally blew it. There is so much about a father's relationship with his son that involves honor, and I had betrayed it. They had been so proud of me.

And now my mom, my dad, and my brothers were all embarrassed. I had let down everybody who believed in me.

I was at the absolute worst point in my life. I was defeated. I wasn't answering anybody's phone calls. I had disappeared. I was incapacitated by the events swirling around me. I didn't know what to do. I was just basically cowering in the corner.

Then the news got worse. The Miami Organized Crime Bureau, a team of state and federal prosecutors, wanted to question me. What would come of that? What would they ask? And knowing that everything I said to them would become public, what should I say? Do I just start babbling and tell them everything I ever did and saw, or do I only respond to questions pertaining to potential illegalities? I really didn't know, but I knew that the wrong words would make me unemployable for good.

I returned home, but was still tearing myself apart, so I decided to go to my church, Our Lady of the Lakes. I just wanted to pray over it. As I entered the church on a weekday around dusk, I found the door open, but it was empty. I let myself in. And I sat on one of those pews where I'd often prayed with my family and friends.

The life-sized statue of Jesus hung on the wall above the altar.

"What should I do? I've never been in a situation like this, what should I do?" I asked, as if forcing the Jesus statue to answer me. "C'mon, damn it, I need your guidance."

As I sat there alone for more than an hour hoping and praying, I kept trying to gain the wisdom to overcome the mess I had created for myself. Finally, I got up to leave. But as I was walking back toward the exit, I noticed there was a door that seemed to creak open. It could have been the wind. It could have been anything. But I took it as an invitation to enter.

It was a confessional, where Catholics go for redemption from their sins. But there was no priest there. There was only a scriptural manual that priests used to counsel parishioners who come before them to confess their sins. I had walked in the wrong door; I had entered through the priest's corridor. I was on his side of the small room, rather than the corner where the parishioners sit.

I looked down at the manual, which was filled with notes for priests and biblical quotes; and there as big as life was the answer to the question I had been asking. The words that would fill me with the confidence to walk into the interrogation room in downtown Miami the next day with my head held reasonably high. It read from Mark 12:17: "Render to Caesar the things that are Caesar's, and to God the things that are God's."

It answered my questions. I wanted to know how much I should divulge. Do I only tell the government prosecutors the information they need to make a case, or do I tell them all my embarrassing sins? My drinking and carousing, my long nights partying, the brawls I witnessed and engaged in, all my stupid youthful indiscretions, which would surely end up the next morning in the pages of the *Miami Herald*, or do I just tell them what they need?

I asked and I received. And to this day, I believe God answered my prayer. Some of you may call that karma or coincidence or even foolishness, believe what you want; I know what I believe.

The next day, prosecutors laid into me. They bullied, screamed, accused, and threatened me with everything they had. It was their job. I was scared, but not intimidated. Under my breath, I kept repeating to myself what I had read in church the previous evening. It carried me through the interrogation. I felt God's hand guiding me through it. I told them everything I knew about San Pedro's associations, his dealings, and his boasts, which turned out to be exactly what they already knew. I gave to Caesar what was Caesar's and then finally heard the words "you're free to leave."

Jan Fisher was a fellow reporter at my TV station. He was a Kentucky guy with a mop of blond hair, a handsome smile, and a real Southern drawl. He came to visit the day after my interrogation. "You're a talented reporter; you should stay and fight your way back on the air." He was worried about me and didn't want me staying alone in my town house, so he practically moved in.

"I know what you're thinking; I know what you're thinking about doing. And I'm not going to let you do it. I'm not going to leave your house until you pull yourself back together."

He stayed by my side and lifted my spirits, but the rest of our colleagues didn't let up. The stories continued, as did the insinuations. Finally, I hit the road again.

I drove and drove, finally ending up Chicago, where I met up with my agents, Saul Foos and Lisa Miller, who I thought had given up on me. Instead, they took me in, gave me a place to sleep at night in their homes, and allowed me to hang out in their office by day.

One day, out of the blue a news director called from KHOU in Houston. Chip Moody, the longtime anchor there, had cancer, and would have to be replaced immediately.

They were looking for a young male anchor who could tell good stories. They needed somebody with Moody's easy delivery who was preferably Hispanic. Wow!

Foos and Miller sent KHOU my résumé tape and two days later got a response.

"Well, you know, we like him. He's talented. His tapes are fantastic. He looks like he's a good writer, with good delivery. He's the full package. But this thing with San Pedro in Miami just doesn't look good. And it doesn't even look like we know what the deal is here. We want to take your word for it, but we don't know."

My agent told me, "If we can somehow convince them you're not tainted by the San Pedro thing, I can get them to hire you as a Monday through Friday anchor." But how do I do that?

Finally, it hit me. I did the only thing I was convinced would get the general manager of KHOU to trust me. I called Janet Reno's right-hand man, a prosecutor who was one of the few who had treated me fairly during my interrogation.

"Look," I told him. "All I want to do is get my life back together again. If you guys are going to charge me with something, charge me. You've heard all the tapes. If you don't think I should even try to get into television anymore, because this is going to keep popping up, tell me. But if not, can you do me a favor? Can you pick up the phone and call this number and talk to this general manager in Houston, and just tell him the truth. I'll live with whatever you say." Then I told him, "And this conversation never took place. I'll know if it happened or didn't when I hear from KHOU."

I don't know what he said. And I'm not revealing his name to protect his integrity, but whatever it was got me one hell of a job at KHOU. I was to become the five o'clock anchor, where I would start to rebuild my career step by step, and much more carefully.

But there was still something missing. *Me!* I still felt like a beaten man, a screwup. I was told I was talented, but I still felt tainted.

I arrived in Houston a couple of days before I was supposed to start work, and I was staying in a hotel downtown. I was anxious about what would happen. I was afraid that everyone who looked at me would be thinking, "Oh, yeah. You're that tainted guy. You're that reporter I just read about in the *Houston Chronicle* from Miami who was involved in some kind of organized crime thing." That's what I saw when I looked in the mirror, so that's all I expected others would see.

Interestingly enough, that first morning in Houston, the first thing I saw in the newspaper was the name San Pedro. It scared the living hell out of me. I thought, "Oh, my God. I know what it's going to say. It's going to say, 'New anchor hired by CBS affiliate has ties to San Pedro.'"

It was April 1, 1986, and the headline in the paper was indeed about San Pedro from Miami. But it wasn't that San Pedro, it was another. Enrique San Pedro was a beloved Catholic priest who spoke four languages and had spent many years in the jungles of Vietnam helping the poor after the war. Archbishop Enrique San Pedro died in 1994. As of this writing, he is in the process of being beatified by the Catholic Church in Rome. Here's what the Houston papers said on the day I arrived: "Houston gets new bishop from Miami, Enrique San Pedro." I don't know if he was indeed a saint, but for me on that day, it's as if God had sent me a guardian angel. I had to find him in the coming weeks and reach out to him.

In the meantime, I looked out my hotel window and I saw this magnificent church. I said to myself, "You know what? That's what I need to do first. I need to go to church and just sit and pray and collect my thoughts."

Somehow, though, walking through the streets of downtown, I got lost and disoriented. The church I saw from the twentieth floor of my hotel was nowhere in sight. Down on the street, nothing looked as it did from my hotel room balcony. Houston is a city made of metal and glass, and when the sun hits it, it feels like you're in a maze.

Eventually, I came across another church. It looked more like a mission. I didn't know exactly what it was, but it was beautiful with a long manicured garden surrounding a Mexican tiled walkway that led to some steps and a porch. I remember swinging the gate open and walking up the steps. I was hoping to find someone who would help me find the church I seemed to have lost.

Suddenly, out of the blue, this gentleman in an open shirt approaches me and asks, "Can I help you?" There was something special about him. He seemed very much at ease. He was wearing a white short-sleeved shirt and black pants.

He said, "You're Rick Sanchez."

"Yes, I am," I answered. "How'd you know?"

"I am from Miami. I just got into town. My name is Enrique San Pedro," he said.

If you're getting goose bumps as you read this, so was I on that day.

I had to think that God had somehow led me to this man. How else does that happen? I know there's such a thing as coincidence, but how does it happen that here's this one man, a fellow Cuban from Miami, last name San Pedro, standing before me as I'm facing the most troubling, the most lonely moment of my life, arriving in a new town where I know that everyone's going to be looking at me and judging me? And just when I needed spiritual guidance the most, there he was. The priest I had not found at Our Lady of the Lakes in Miami, I had found by accident, or intervention, at the Archdiocese of Houston. And not just any priest. I had found in a city of 5 million people the priest who is now being considered for sainthood by the church of my ancestors. Can you say divine intervention?

We prayed together. I cried. I called my mother. I told him how awful I felt about myself. He lifted me up. And he gave me, in many ways, the conviction and the strength to go on. He shared with me his motto: "Go gladly and spend yourself on what is right, and leave to God what you may see as wrong." Then he said, "I will spend myself for your sake as well." He did. And I will never forget his words, nor his kindness.

Nuke 'Em All

I believe in God, because of what God has done for me. My relationship with God is very real. It's not based on politics, or ego, or expediency; it's personal. And it's now an important part of why I succeed as a man, as a husband to the only woman I love and hope to spend the rest of my life with, and to my four children, who provide me more joy and fulfillment than any drink or night out on the town could ever compete with.

I believe that there is something more powerful than us watching over all of us. My faith has guided me through the darkest periods of my life, and it has stayed with me. As a Christian, I believe in the teachings of Jesus Christ. I teach my children my faith. We pray together every night at dinner and I've always sent them to Christian schools to learn the ways of our faith.

So for me to suddenly look at Christians in my own community and question their motives is painful, but true.

When I arrived in Atlanta, I was hoping to be able to go to church with my family as we have always done. I've never been completely hung up on the idea that I have to go to a Catholic church. My family and I, we've belonged to Baptist churches, and to nondenominational churches. I just like the serenity of being in church with my wife and children.

But I found that when I got to Atlanta in 2003–04, right at the height of the Iraq War, there was suddenly something different about going to church.

Walking through the parking lot on my way to church in my suburban community, I saw bumper sticker after bumper sticker proclaiming almost an allegiance to causes that seemed to represent politics more than faith. But it seemed to go beyond that, with something even my kids picked up on.

There were bumper stickers proclaiming support for policies that were not exactly in keeping with the teachings of Jesus Christ, at least not the "prince of peace and love" that I believed in.

Many of them had funny phrases about people on "welfare," others talked about "illegals" and reminded them to "speak English, you're in America." Still others mocked "global warming," and almost every other car bumper sticker seemed to suggest we should "nuke 'em." "Nuke who?" I thought.

> love thy neighbor no longer seems to apply :-(

> Agree. Those messages must sadden God's heart.

> not to be flip, but you're going to the wrong church.

Fact is, as my children noted, we saw more signs about political policy than we did about supporting Christianity. And inside the church, the pastor's message sounded at times more like a Rush Limbaugh radio show than a sermon. What was going on?

Was church for these parishioners more about worshiping GOD or the GOP? It was bothersome—it's not that I couldn't see how some people could agree with their messages. After all, as I mentioned earlier, I have voted for Republicans and Democrats on several occasions. It's just that it seemed intolerant, particularly for those who say they are devotees of Christianity.

■ "When the Wicked Beareth Rule"

It came to a head for me in 2008.

There's a little church about three blocks from our house that I have to drive by every morning on the way to work. It's a pretty little town, Tyrone, Georgia. It was settled by the Irish in the years after the potato famine, and recently the city leaders asked me to be their St. Patrick's Day Parade grand marshal. The Crestwood Baptist Church sits on a corner overlooking the railroad tracks.

The week before the election between McCain and Obama, the

polls showed Obama was heading toward an all but certain victory. I noticed the marquee in front of the church had an odd message. I was taken aback by it. It read: "When the wicked beareth rule, the people mourn. Proverbs 29:2."

Well, given my experiences in the community, it seemed obvious, an obvious reference to a likely Obama election victory. I thought I knew what that pastor was trying to say: He was almost telling his flock to go out and vote for anybody but Obama.

I thought it was outrageous. So I took a picture of it. And I put the story on TV that day. I asked the pastor if he would come on to talk to me about it on air, but he wouldn't. His public relations people responded with a statement claiming the pastor regretted having put up the sign, but that I had taken it wrong. Their position was that he was merely encouraging people to vote, not telling them who to vote for—and certainly not suggesting that either of the candidates was wicked.

That wasn't the way it struck me, nor hundreds of my viewers, who seemed to catch the pastor's drift. I was left with a sense that the sign was deliberately suggesting something sinister about the Democratic candidate with that oddly foreign-sounding name.

I wondered why a church pastor would feel the need to engage in political messages, especially one with such a sharp edge: "wicked," really?

But I would soon find out this was tame compared to what was to follow. More signs directed at Obama, at church after church, on billboard after billboard and bumper sticker after bumper sticker.

These are not just private thoughts. These are signs they put on their marquees, in front of their churches, for everybody to see. It was almost as if there was a movement within the church to sway people to vote against Obama.

After the election, even more signs started cropping up. For me, as a Christian, and for many on my staff and many of you, it seemed both revealing and startling. I did a story about it on my show.

A pastor in Jonesville, South Carolina, put up a sign that said, "Obama, Osama. Hmm, are they brothers?"

When NBC asked Pastor Roger Byrd, the guy who put it up, if he thought Obama was Muslim, the pastor said, "I don't know. See, it asks a question: Are they brothers? In other words, is he Muslim? I don't know. He says he's not. I hope he's not. But I don't know. And it's just something to try to stir people's minds. It was never intended to hurt feelings or to offend anybody."

That was his explanation. Then there was the sign outside a church in Wichita, Kansas, where the marquee read, "America, we have a Muslim president. This is sin against the Lord."

I called Pastor Mark Holick and invited him on the show. He boasted to me that yes, he put it up.

"Why are you saying that Barack Obama is a Muslim if he has repeatedly said that he's not a Muslim?" I asked him.

Then I offered this example. "Let me read to you what Barack Obama says . . . 'I am a Christian, so I have a deep faith. I'm rooted in the Christian tradition. I believe that there are many paths to the same place. And that is a belief that there is a higher power—a belief that we are connected as a people.'"

I pointed out to Pastor Holick that the president said he's a Christian, but may be allowing people of other faiths to find their own path. Then I asked him what was wrong with the president's message.

Holick told me the president was wrong to suggest you could go to heaven if you're not a Christian. He even seemed to be suggesting that only Americans would go to heaven.

I then reminded him that Pope John Paul II and Billy Graham both suggested there are other acceptable paths to heaven, and that as president, Obama had to defend our nation's founding principles of separation between church and state. His response, "That's not in the Constitution." "Back to that," I thought.

> I'd like to see that guy's face when he realizes Jesus wasn't American.

> People are so strange in their beliefs. Really so few "Christians" understand the teachings of Christ.

"How can a pastor, who's supposed to be a man of God, be so quick to judge?" I thought. I'm not here to defend President Obama, or anyone else, for that matter, but does he really deserve to be judged or accused, especially by a man who calls himself a minister?

W-W-J-D?

When you really listen to what extremists espouse, you just have to ask: Is it what Jesus would espouse?

You don't have to be a Sunday school teacher to know that Jesus Christ wasn't exactly a fan of giving to the rich instead of the poor.

When I hear churchgoing Americans in my neighborhood talk about "those lazy people on welfare, or those Mexicans who are trying to take everything away from us," I'm left to wonder.

> Jesus would say, in all his profound simplicity, that sick people cannot be ignored.

> Jesus would demand affordable health care for all!

> "Verily I say unto you, Inasmuch as ye have done it

unto one of the least of . . . my brethren, ye have
done it unto me."

How can you be for the guy who says you should always turn the other cheek and then have a bumper sticker that says "Just nuke 'em all"? You think that's Jesus's solution to foreign policy? To want to bomb the people without taking into account the country's history, culture, or needs seems egoistic, not godly. It is at the very least difficult to reconcile with Jesus's teachings.

And by the way, speaking of "nuke 'em all," what about the children of countries we engage militarily? What about the moms and grandmas? What about people who may not have agreed with the policies of those leaders who we don't like?

Saddam, Our Guy, WMD and All

Let's take Saddam Hussein, for example. The evidence now shows we bolstered and supported him during much of the Reagan administrations. Why? Because of Iran, with whom they were at war. Iran was for the United States a geopolitical counterweight.

But I'm not talking about just having relations with Iraq for the sake of geopolitical convenience. I'm talking about what is detailed now in countless interviews and articles, including one that appeared in the *Washington Post* in December 2002, about our government supplying Saddam Hussein, through a Chilean business used as a front, with cluster bombs that he would eventually use against his enemies.

My job as a journalist is to make you think. If I have you thinking, that's good. Here's more to think about. When Saddam Hussein was using mustard gas on more than 100,000 Iranians, we not only supported him, we seemed to be giving him the encouragement to do so.

On August 18, 2002, the *New York Times* carried a front-page story headlined "Officers Say U.S. Aided Iraq Despite the Use of Gas." The article quotes anonymous U.S. "senior military officers," who say that during the 1980s, the Reagan administration covertly provided "critical battle planning assistance at a time when American intelligence knew that Iraqi commanders would employ chemical weapons in waging the decisive battles of the Iran-Iraq war."

Thoughtful, honest students of American foreign policy on both the left and the right have a tough time morally squaring this.

William Safire was a well-respected author, speechwriter, and conservative *New York Times* columnist. Listen to what he seemed compelled to write on December 7, 1992: "Iraqgate is uniquely horrendous: a scandal about the systematic abuse of power by misguided leaders of three democratic nations [the United States, Britain, and Italy] to secretly finance the arms buildup of a dictator." That's no lefty saying that; that's Safire, a hawk.

That's nuance, that's valuable information. Those are the stories that put wars in perspective. They are the stories you share with me and I share with my children, just as my father shared his stories and his knowledge. It doesn't make me, or my children, unpatriotic for asking why so many cars in the church parking lot say "nuke 'em all." In fact, it makes us better Americans, more informed Americans. We are asking the questions Jesus would have asked.

Family Values and All Show, No Go

I love my children and I want them to have a religious foundation, a Christian foundation. I pray every night at dinner with my children, and I teach them to pray and to express themselves through God. I love my wife and I consider her the rock of our family, just as my mother was in my boyhood home.

That's family values. Family values are important to most of us. But is it about politics, or is it personal?

Radio talk-show hosts use the veneer of "family values" to attract listeners, just as politicians on both sides of the aisle brag about their "religiousness" to get votes. However, a funny thing has been happening to many of them once they get in office that makes many of us ask: "This is the guy who was telling me how to live my life?"

The Republican governor of South Carolina was a family-values politician who moralized about his faith and public policy, until he was found out to be lying about walking the Appalachian Trail when he was actually in Argentina with a woman who wasn't his wife.

Former North Carolina Democratic senator John Edwards was romantically linked to his own staff member while he was running for president. His wife was battling cancer at the time. He finally admitted to fathering a child with his staff cinematographer.

Larry Craig, the Republican senator from Idaho, more often than not voted along a staunch "traditional values" platform, until he was caught in a bathroom stall allegedly playing footsies with another man and ended up having to explain away why he was arrested.

Democratic congressman Eric Massa found himself on my "list you don't want to be on" after he resigned his position under a cloud of public accusations that he was making advances toward his male staff members. While he became the subject of a congressional ethics investigation and an FBI probe, Massa said he did not approve a payment of $40,000 to a staff member and that the "groping" allegations were misconstrued.

Republican congressman Mark Foley from Florida, according to our own reporting, was literally propositioning young male pages who worked in the halls of Capitol Hill. These were young men who were sent by their parents to learn how their government works, and he was caught sending them e-mails and apparently having phone conversations with them that were, at the very least, questionable. Foley resigned in disgrace.

Then there's Republican senator John Ensign of Nevada, who admitted having a long-running affair with a campaign staffer—who happened to be married to his chief of staff, with whom he attended church—until he was called out. Who called him out? His chief of staff and best friend, who accused Ensign of trying to buy him off with a lobbying job, which got the attention of the Justice Department and the Senate Ethics Committee. My interview with the senator remains what many would call his only live broadcast challenge on the record to this day.

▓ Killing Tiller

Why do some religious leaders want to strip away the concept of separation of church and state? When you read through the Jeffersonian and Madisonian dicta, it's clear that our forefathers wanted to establish the privacy of religion among individuals in the United States. You could worship as you choose. You could believe what you believe.

But no single issue seems to stir the religious passions, if not the hatred of Americans, more than the issue of abortion and *Roe v. Wade*. It's a reasonable issue to question, no matter which side of the argument you may come from. But when it's approached from the point of view of hatred, rarely does anything good come from it. And hatred, as we all know, all too often leads to violence.

On Memorial Day in 2009, a man took the law into his own hands and gunned down the abortion provider George Tiller at a church in Wichita, Kansas. Tiller was no stranger to controversy. He had been the target of protests for most of the thirty-six years that he performed abortions. His clinic, which performed questionable, but legal, late-term abortions, had been bombed, and he had been shot before, in both arms, in an attack in 1993.

He had also gained the attention of many a talk-show host and pundit, who referred to him as "Tiller the baby killer."

His death, however, sparked outrage on both sides of the issue. David N. O'Steen, the director of the National Right to Life Committee, immediately issued a statement that said the group "unequivocally condemns any such acts of violence regardless of motivation."

That wasn't the universal view, though. Randall Terry, the founder of the antiabortion group Operation Rescue, said: "We grieve for him that he did not have time to properly prepare his soul to face God. I am more concerned that the Obama administration will use Tiller's killing to intimidate pro-lifers into surrendering our most effective rhetoric and actions." He exhorted his followers to continue to "peacefully protest them at their offices and homes, and yes, even their churches."

The Southern Baptist minister and radio host Wiley S. Drake was more blunt. "I am glad that he is dead," he said.

Religious zealotry takes many forms. And although we often report it as international news developments, it also happens in our own backyard. I reported extensively on the story of the psychiatrist Major Nidal Hasan, accused of opening fire on fellow soldiers at Fort Hood on November 5, killing thirteen and wounding thirty others. He was shot by a civilian law enforcement officer and is paralyzed from the waist down. He is currently being held at Bell County Jail in Benton, Texas, awaiting trial.

Do we not pay enough attention or see the signs of religious zealots who could be potentially dangerous? Since the high-profile shooting incident, investigators have found that Hasan was promoted despite supervisors' concerns about his extremist views on Islam and odd behavior. Reports also suggest holding officers accountable in the future for not adequately reporting issues regarding Hasan and allowing him to move up in the ranks despite poor performance reviews.

The report also found supervisors "don't want to rock the boat" and prevent junior officers from getting promoted.

Lesson learned? We hope.

Dangerous Words

You were appalled by the comments of Pastor Steven Anderson, who delivered a hateful and seemingly threatening sermon in Phoenix, Arizona. The sermon was delivered on the eve of the president's arrival in Phoenix. On that Sunday, Anderson told his parishioners that Obama deserved to die—that "he wanted Obama's children to be fatherless."

He went on to holler out in church that Michelle Obama should "become a widow" and her husband should "melt like a snail."

He explained his threatening comments about the president of the United States this way: "I have to say these things because this is what the Bible is telling me to say."

Here's the part that gets really scary. One of the parishioners that day at his church was a fellow named Chris. And the next day, after hearing his pastor suggest "Obama should die," Chris shows up at the convention center in Phoenix—where the president was scheduled to speak—with an AR-15 rifle over his shoulder.

Now, thank goodness, nothing happened. But when Chris was interviewed by reporters outside the convention center, he said that he's willing to resort to forceful resistance against the government. You called that scary stuff.

Bottom line is those types of incidents are just a little too close for comfort when it comes to the security of the U.S. president. And also a little too close, a little too reminiscent of the very thing we've witnessed overseas when religious zealots take down leaders, like the Islamic fundamentalists who assassinated the Egyptian leader Anwar

Sadat—or the orthodox Jewish fundamentalist who assassinated Yit-zhak Rabin.

I interviewed an agent with the Secret Service who told me they were concerned about the incident with Chris and would question Anderson about it, but in general they seemed to regard Anderson as a crackpot. Most Americans hope they are right.

I also reached out to Anderson, but I did not interview him on my show. I thought about it. But in the end, I decided not to give him a national showcase for his hate.

Dangerous Thinking

I've learned that hate, like religion, comes in many denominations.

Pastor Anderson wishes death upon the president of the United States as part of a Sunday sermon. The Reverend Fred Phelps leads his squads of followers from the Westboro Baptist Church to spread hate and inflict pain across the country.

I brought Phelps on my show to explain himself after a group of Westboro's parishioners chose to protest at a funeral for a dead soldier who had just been flown back from Iraq.

As this family tried to bury their son, the protesters shouted that he deserved to die because of gays. Gays?

That's what I asked Phelps. But here's how he fired back:

"For goodness' sakes, all it was was a protestation against the gov-ernment of the United States who's against the word of God," he said. "They don't want me preaching that God is punishing America by killing those servicemen, and if that's how he's doing it and sending them home in body bags, then the appropriate form of choice would be their funerals. And there's nothing wrong with preaching respect-fully at a great distance from the funeral when it's going on."

When I pressed him, he lumped me in with the rest of the antagonists he sees as part of the conspiracy against him and his merry band of religious zealots. "You're just a hysterical nincompoop, like all the rest of them. This is the First Amendment—what you ought to be worried about is the loss of First Amendment rights in the United States for which those guys claim they're over there fighting."

It didn't make much sense, and I wish we could just dismiss it. But Phelps's small, but loud band of followers continues their protests across the nation and, sadly, continue spreading what you all roundly describe as their seeds of hate.

President, or Antichrist Beast Who Teaches Fornication?

I thought I was done with the Phelps clan, but I wasn't. In the fall of 2009, they protested outside the school the president's daughters attend. I mentioned it on my show, and said that traditionally, the president's children were off-limits.

That brought an angry response from Phelps's wife, via e-mail, that stunned both me and my executive producer Angie Massie, an Ohio native with no tolerance for zealots.

Here's what the nice Mrs. Phelps wrote:

"Rick says the president's daughters are 'off limits,'" she wrote. "Apparently not for him to fawn and coo over, but for anyone else who has some words for them and the rest of the youth of this nation that pertain to God and obedience.

"Listen up, Rick! You do all that hysterical crying on your program, and you change NOTHING. Antichrist Beast Obama has promised to the world that if his daughters—whom he and this society will teach to fornicate—become pregnant, he will see to it that his grandbabies are murdered in the womb. Where is your outrage about them being taught that God-awful soul-damning lie?

"Antichrist Beast Obama has promised to be a 'fierce advocate' for sodomites. His children get a steady diet of that lie. That's why when we picketed outside those schools one of the girls' fellow students had a sign saying, 'I kissed a girl and I liked it.' That's what you're teaching these children. And that's just ducky with your she-man backside."

Wait. It's still not over.

"This nation is doomed. It's too late! The only hope for any single soul is to come out from among this filthy nation and OBEY GOD. Those girls and all their fellow students are as entitled to that only message of hope as much as the rest of the children in this country. They're old enough to be raped by priests and rabbis. They're old enough to be taught it's OK to be gay by the sodomite education czar who will teach that message aggressively to kindergarteners."

Here comes the punch line.

"So they're old enough to hear the truth of God. And they DO NOT get a pass because their dad is the evil antichrist! Obama hates this nation. He's a Muslim."

The e-mail went on, but there it was again: See the pattern? "He's a Muslim." I'd love to dismiss it as the ranting of a crazy woman, but you and many Americans have a hard time ignoring that recurring theme.

You think those are isolated incidents I've come across? Well, here's another example of a pastor off the deep end who I wish I could ignore.

His name is Tony Alamo, and as I described it on my show, "he's been accused of trafficking underage girls across state lines for sex. Now, we have been monitoring his trial and have seen a parade of women come forward to say they were forced to marry him when they were just little girls. By the way, they also say their parents looked the other way because they were a part of it."

When I asked him about it, he said the Bible viewed the age of consent as puberty. He never admitted to any of the government's allegations, but he said, "That means when a woman is able to conceive, and have a child, she is an adult and she could be married. But we don't do that at our church. We never have." Really, let's see what happens at his trial.

I'm not including this here because of his bizarre biblical interpretations. It's what he said after that. As we continued our conversation, he pulled out the same accusation that is reverberating through Christian churches across the country.

"You're part of the government regime to try to destroy Christianity," he said. And he later added, "You're not a nation of laws. You are the Antichrist."

Fact, I am not the Antichrist, but I am anti–religious zealots and I do believe they are dangerous. And apparently so did a jury of like-minded Americans, who found him guilty of taking girls as young as nine across state lines for sex. He will spend the rest of his life behind bars.

I, like you, wish we could dismiss these guys as the lunatic fringe, but can we?

> if a pastor wants someone dead then it seems they are doing someone else's work, not God's.

> Yet another "Christian" seeking to kill someone who differs in opinion. Baaaaaad! Christianity has lost its meaning.

> He's no better than Bin Laden—inciting people to kill others.

We have to ask ourselves this question: Let's suppose that instead of it being Pastor Steven Anderson speaking the day before President Obama arrived, let's suppose it was an imam at a local mosque saying about George W. Bush, "George Bush deserves to die. His children should be fatherless. His wife should be a widow. And I want to see George Bush melt like a snail. And I'm praying that he dies and goes to hell."

Imagine that an imam had said that. Would we have not been outraged? Point is, as wrongheaded and dangerous as we may think some of our enemies overseas are, we should remember there are also enemies at home. Our mission, my mission at CNN, is to investigate both.

CHAPTER 8

You're Sick of Anti-Immigration Hysteria

failed first grade because I was retarded! What do you think of that, huh? I guess the word "retarded" must have been much less politically incorrect back then, because that's what Mrs. McCalvane wrote on my transcript. My mother cried. Hell, I cried. I was six. Wouldn't you? Talk about a stigma.

Was I retarded? No, not really. It's just that I didn't speak even a lick of English. And I was among the first in the wave of Cuban immigrants to come to Miami, so Mrs. McCalvane didn't know what to make of me. I was a scared little boy in the back of the class making strange noises. It was 1966, and my teacher, a courtly Southern woman, had never dealt with an immigrant student, so she assumed there must be something wrong with me. In fact, I was speaking Spanish. It's all I knew. So, yes, English really is my second language.

It's funny. I was always too embarrassed to tell that story. Today, the shame is gone, because I understand it's part of the immigrant experience.

I'm not embarrassed, and I'm not bitter. I'm proud. Those experiences give me a unique and, I think, valuable perspective not shared by many people in my business.

Through it all, I only learned to love this country more for the opportunities and freedoms it gave me and my family. Like all immigrants, I cherish the American ideal, those things this country stands for. And like all immigrants, I hold up a mirror in which this country can see a reflection of itself—in its entire splendor, and with all its flaws, I love this place.

Treating Me Like a Dog

Let me begin with my first lessons in bigotry.

None is more memorable than the one I learned the summer of my junior year in high school. The trip to Boca Raton from Hialeah was so long, I fell asleep in the back of the enclosed cargo hold. Yep, it was a three-mover trip and J&M Cabinet Makers' only truck was unbearably hot, even in the non-air-conditioned cabin. So you can imagine what the cargo hold was like, sealed up under the South Florida sun, bouncing over every pothole along the three-hour trip to Boca.

To us, Boca was a place where the lives of the rich and famous Floridians are on display. And I was proud that my dad and I were chosen to make the big delivery.

I knew we'd arrived when I was shaken by the sound of the sliding door being raised and heard my father's hearty laugh. "Look at my son," he said to his stunned coworker. "Ave Maria, he's fast asleep in the cargo hold, not a worry in the world."

Then it was time to get to work, meticulously unloading and carefully carrying each piece of the kitchen and bathroom cabinets through the house—making sure we didn't damage anything inside the house itself.

Did I say house? I mean mansion. It was huge, with giant columns framing a porte cochere that was tall enough to drive our truck through. Of course, we didn't do that. We parked on the street and schlepped the cabinets for half a football field to the house.

It took an hour, but we finished the job. The good news is we had managed to carefully place each item in the house without a scratch.

The bad news was that I was on the verge of heat stroke. Four hours baking in the cargo hold and lifting and carrying cabinets had taken their toll. Surely, the home owner, the bleached-blonde, 1970s miniskirted wife of some successful guy, I assumed, would reward us with something cold to drink, right?

Not exactly!

My father's English is made up of about fifty words. So I jumped in and asked the home owner if she could offer us something to drink. My father would never have asked—not that he didn't want it. It's just that he figured if people didn't have the *educación* to offer it themselves, it wasn't his place to ask.

Here's a quick Spanish lesson: *Educación* doesn't mean education. It's one of the most important words in Spanish, and it means the exact same thing from the coast of Spain to the tip of Argentina to the barrios of Miami: It means decency.

But I figured it wouldn't hurt to ask for something to drink.

The woman looked at me and pointed to the backyard, to a spigot with a muddy water hose attached. With my head down, I thanked her and walked outside and drank the water from the garden hose as fast as I could. I still felt sick and wanted to throw up when I was done. Maybe it was from drinking too fast, or maybe it was from the demoralizing dejection I felt from being treated like an animal and being forced to drink water from a dirty garden hose.

On the trip back I squeezed into the cabin with my dad and his fellow mover, and I asked my father how a person could be so rude. His answer stays with me to this day:

He told me I should be grateful.

"How should I be grateful to somebody who wouldn't even offer me a drink?" I asked.

"She's rich," he said, "and to her *tu eres un perro*, you are a dog." He went on to tell me how often he had been treated that way and how fortunate I was to experience it and see it for myself.

Still puzzled, I asked, "But how did she do me a favor?"

"Now you know," he answered, "why you need to study and go to college, why you need to become somebody in America, a professional, and not be a *perro* like me."

I get sad as I recall and write this story. Not that I feel bad for myself, but rather for my dad and all the other immigrants and poor workers who've experienced similar treatment.

By the way, that most likely would include your grandparents, or your parents, or maybe you.

Almost all of us here trace our roots to someplace else.

America's present immigration policy is described as broken. And few disagree with the fact that it has to be fixed. Our borders are much too porous. And we need to establish a policy to decide who should go and who should stay and at what price. Most Americans seem to agree on that. But agreeing and finding a solution are two very different things, especially when attempts to solve the problem become mired by political emotional, overheated rhetoric on either side.

Illegal immigration started with Columbus.

Historically most nativists are bigots. That hasn't changed.

Some Nativists are bigots. Some have legitimate concerns. Immigrants should obey the law.

They are hypocrites who benefit from illegal immigrants in this country. I do not miss Lou Dobbs.

Send them all back!

Here's some historical perspective. Much of what many Americans say about Mexicans and other Hispanics, describing them as intruders and outsiders, is no different than what was said in the past about the Germans, the Irish, the Italians, the Jews, the Poles, the Swedes, and the Norwegians, just to name a few. It's part of our history. And experts say that history has proven again and again that immigrant groups assimilate as English-speaking Americans within two generations. And they say it's happening now again.

Before we get too far into the weeds of those statistics, let me just use myself and my brothers as examples. We were born to parents who never learned to speak English, yet we all speak English as our primary language. I learned it well enough to become among the first bilingual, Spanish-English, American network anchors. Does it make me unique? Maybe in broadcasting, but there are millions like me, just like there were millions before who spoke English-Italian, or English-German, or English-Norwegian for one generation. Now I wish I could pass Spanish along to my kids. Trust me, I try, but it's tough. Getting them to speak Spanish is like trying to hold back a rushing wave; no matter how much you try and resist the natural flow, it eventually consumes them.

FAIR is the Federation for American Immigration Reform, an organization of citizens who want the nation's immigration policies reformed.

By the way, let me state unequivocally, I have enjoyed interviewing members of FAIR about how to fix the immigration problem. And the stated goals on their Web site seem perfectly legitimate: "FAIR seeks to improve border security, to stop illegal immigration, and to promote immigration levels consistent with the national interest—more traditional rates of about 300,000 a year."

They are in favor of a comprehensive reform strategy, and its members whom I have interviewed go about discussing it earnestly and vigorously. Let me emphasize once again: To cast a wide net and say that anyone involved in the anti-immigration movement or even anyone involved in FAIR is a bigoted xenophobe, as some of their critics charge, is neither fair nor true. Their point of view may seem harsh to some, but that doesn't mean they all espouse the extreme positions.

The Black Experience

Some observers of political trends argue that some of the tactics used against immigrants today are akin to what took place in the United States in the 1960s during the battle over civil rights. Remember "states' rights"? Historians say it was a political strategy employed during the administration of Richard Nixon to win over the mostly Democratic South during the 1960s. Ask any black person who lived through the era and they'll tell you exactly what it means. They say it was a simple principle: divide through fear.

"States' rights" to its critics was a buzzword, from a political standpoint a very effective buzzword, which really meant "antiblack" or "white rights." But to its supporters then and now, it's a kind of call to action to keep the federal government from interfering in local and state affairs.

And unfortunately, in many ways, that may be part of the political climate revolving around the immigration debate.

Not everybody who has a strong position on immigration and thinks that we need to control our borders is xenophobic—hardly! It's that often the loudest voices are. Those loud voices take the public position that they believe immigrants need to come to the United States legally, which is agreed upon by almost all Americans. But then some take it a step further and also argue that these "illegal" immigrants are deteriorating the way of life here for traditional Americans.

Their critics say that's a purely nativist viewpoint: That they worry too many immigrants are changing the face of America, and they want to keep America just as it is.

Most anti-illegal-immigration activists are not nativists worried about keeping America as it is. Many of them simply point out that illegal immigrants are driving down wages, overburdening our schools and hospitals, and not paying their share of taxes. Those are all reasonable arguments we've covered at length on CNN.

They are valid concerns for all of us but felt mostly by Americans living in border states and pockets throughout the country experiencing the brunt of immigration.

Would you want to live in a low-income community where many immigrants congregate and where services become overwhelmed?

Would you want your children to go to a public school where more than half the kids in their classes don't yet speak any English?

Would you want to live in a community where if you have to go to the emergency room you find that you're in line behind one hundred people, because none of them have health insurance and whenever they get sick that's the only place they can go?

Those are the frustrations regarding the immigration issue felt directly by some Americans living in regions where illegal immigration populations are most concentrated.

And it would be disingenuous to write about this topic without dealing with those concerns honestly, by recognizing it's a reality.

Is it a new phenomenon? Most historians would say absolutely not. Cities or regions with heavy concentrations of immigrants who make other groups feel put upon and resentful is not a today story, it's part of the American story.

It's occurred again and again in places like Boston, Philadelphia, Los Angeles, Miami, and New York, where I once bought that antique sign that read "Irish Need Not Apply."

It is part of our history, which has tended to highlight our resilience as a nation. Ironically, some of today's loudest anti–illegal immigrant protestors are undoubtedly descendants of yesterday's most disapproved of arrivals. Think about that.

In the long run, history has tended to prove that the melting pot does not boil over. It works. Will it happen again? Let's look at and compare some of those arguments while we examine how the burdens created by immigrants today compare to the contributions of those immigrants.

Crime: Anti–illegal immigration activists suggest that undocumented immigrants are more apt to commit crimes than nonimmigrants in the United States. And it certainly would seem like they're right, with all the media hype that usually surrounds crimes involving an "illegal" suspect.

What are the facts? Here's what FAIR says on its Web site: "Adult illegal aliens represented 3.1 percent of the total adult population of the country in 2003. By comparison, the illegal alien prison population represented a bit more than 4.5 percent of the overall prison population. Therefore, deportable criminal aliens were more than half as likely to be incarcerated as their share of the population."

It's a strong argument, but here's what sociologists in California found about crime and the immigrant population.

Walter Ewing and Ruben Rumbaut's study "The Myth of Immigrant Criminality" finds that violent and property crime rates have dropped 34 percent and 26 percent respectively since 1994. At the same time, the illegal immigrant population doubled to an estimated 12 million.

They say immigrants are simply saddled with this unfairly.

"This myth is not supported by the data and is refuted by empirical data," said Rumbaut, a professor of sociology at UC Irvine, to the *North County Times* in San Diego.

Then there's a report released by the Immigration Policy Center, which is part of a nonprofit group focusing on immigration. It finds that U.S.-born men, ages eighteen to thirty-nine, are five times more likely to be incarcerated than foreign-born men in the same age group. Let me repeat that: Those born in the United States are more likely to commit a crime, five times more likely!

By the way, my experience is that nobody is harsher on immigrant criminals than immigrants themselves. They themselves say round 'em up. And if it's shown they came here with the express purpose of joining a criminal enterprise, there is no equivocation. Deport them. And if they come back into the country, lock them up. That's what you say. And it's what illegal immigrants I've spoken with tell me.

Trust me when I say this: No one is more loathed by hardworking immigrants than those who sully the reputation of those immigrants by committing violent crimes within the country that was kind enough to host them. My dad, and I'm sure yours too, agrees, *"Mira, córtale los huevos."* I can see my dad's index finger scraping across his neck as he says those words, which crudely translated mean "cut his nuts off."

Emergency Rooms: Anti–illegal immigration activists suggest that undocumented immigrants are more apt to use emergency rooms for their medical needs. And certainly if you look at the number of them that are uninsured it would seem to be an accurate assessment.

According to the Pew Hispanic Center, "59% of the nation's illegal immigrants are uninsured, compared with 25% of legal immigrants and 14% of U.S. citizens. That means that illegal immigrants represent about 15% of the nation's 47 million uninsured." However, while they represent a higher percentage of the uninsured, others argue it is not true that they are more apt to use health-care services. In fact, according to the Public Policy Institute of California, where arguably the largest number of undocumented immigrants reside, they are not crowding the state's emergency rooms.

The institute found that foreign-born citizens who are not U.S. citizens are among the least likely to seek treatment in an ER. It goes on to report that "noncitizens (some of whom are presumably undocumented) are less apt to visit an emergency department." And furthermore, it explains that the finding "is consistent with other research showing that the foreign-born, and especially undocumented immigrants, use less medical care and contribute less to health care spending relative to their share of the population."

Schools: Anti-illegal-immigration activists suggest immigrants crowd our schools and can't or refuse to learn English.

While my reporting has shown that some schools in border states are overcrowded, the problem is not nationwide.

Now, let's talk about learning English. As I've learned from reports I've filed from schools in border states, English as a Second Language (or ESL) programs, as they are called, are inefficient. They separate new arrivals from the general enrollment—keeping them in a bilingual setting, often for too long.

However, research seems to indicate it is not true that immigrant students are failing to learn English. In fact, study after study has concluded that today's Hispanic immigrants assimilate and learn English at exactly the same rate as immigrants from the past.

Princeton University sociologists have done extensive research on this topic, and according to their most recent report, Mexican migrants learn English at similar rates as previous immigrants from other parts of the world.

Princeton University professor Alexander Barnard writes in "Myths and Realities of Illegal Immigration" that "although almost 75% of immigrants come with weak English skills, they learn the language quickly after arrival."

And Barnard goes on to find that "by the second generation, 90% of undocumented immigrants speak English very well and more than half prefer English to their native tongue."

How is that different from Italians, Germans, Dutch, or Norwegians? The Princeton study says it's not.

Yet, how many times do you hear stories about people bragging, erroneously but perhaps romantically, about their ancestors being

Americanized the moment they got off the boat? One of the stories, of course, is how they immediately mastered English.

Let me go back to bilingual education because, as I mentioned, it's a part of my own history.

> Bilingual education reinforces segregation. It only benefits people if it truly transitions people into thinking in English.

> bilingual ed. is meant to teach content in 1st lang while learning 2nd language. That's all.

Mrs. McCalvane may have done me a favor. By being immersed in the language, as painful and difficult as it was, I learned to speak English fluently. When I arrived, there was no English as a Second Language program. Trust me, as my life story shows, kids may need help from a bilingual teacher maybe for a semester or two, but after that they are truly better off with a sink-or-swim "immersion" curriculum.

▨ Are Our Ancestors That Different?

It's wonderful to romanticize how different previous generations were. We can make up stories about how our ancestors diligently petitioned the United States for an entry visa and then waited patiently for a reply. That's a great story, but for the most part, it's also not true.

> my ancestors didn't come here thinking they would get hand outs. they worked their bums off, real hard.

> my ancestors went thru the process. They didn't
> come illegally and break the law!
>
> my ancestors waited in line 2 enter U.S. legally.

That all sounds great, but here's what my research has shown. The first limits placed on the number of immigrants allowed in the country occurred in the 1920s. And before the early 1900s, there really was no process for applying to enter the United States legally at all, none! The process simply didn't exist, because immigrants were not processed back then until they actually arrived.

Of the 25 million immigrants who arrived through Ellis Island, only 1 percent was excluded. And those exclusions were based on rare medical conditions. Bottom line: almost everyone who showed up was allowed in.

So it really was a different game altogether back then. The history professor Mae M. Ngai at Columbia University has researched immigration patterns. She says immigrants in the early 1900s provided the same thing many of today's immigrants provide: "cheap, unskilled labor that made possible the nation's industrial and urban expansion. They shoveled pig iron, dug sewers and subway tunnels and sewed shirtwaists. Even then, people born in the U.S. complained that the newcomers stole jobs, were ignorant, criminal and showed no desire to become citizens. The rhetoric was often unabashedly prejudiced against Italians, Jews, Poles and other 'degraded races of Europe.'"

Have you been in a poultry-processing plant lately? Or picked cotton or tomatoes? There are whole families who have come to this country to work under some of the most despicable, disgusting conditions imaginable, and spent decades doing it. They've built their lives, bought homes, watched their kids grow up and start families of their own—and, yes, paid taxes—working at jobs many Americans would find unbearable.

Some argue today's arrivals are fighting the myth or imaginary image we've conjured up about our ancestors. Hispanic activists say to their critics: "Show me the documents your grandfather filled out from overseas, or your great-grandfather filled out from overseas, or your great-great-great-grandfather filled out from overseas that allowed them to arrive 'legally.'" It's a fair point, considering that prior to World War I, except for the infirm and victims of the Chinese Exclusion Act, there were really no pre-arrival "legals" or "illegals."

As for the great-great-great-granddads of most Americans, all they had to do was show up on our shores on a boat, hungry, willing to work, and willing to love America and they were in.

In fact, Hispanic activists make the argument that unlike our ancestors, today's immigrants are actually being asked to come here. That's right!

Here's what I've learned while reporting about this. There is evidence suggesting that some illegal immigrants are recruited by U.S. manufacturers who attract tens of thousands of undocumented immigrants to work in the textile, milling, poultry, and construction industries. And then they're kept on payrolls by being assigned a perfectly legal tax ID number. That number allows the employer to deduct taxes from their salary without having to reveal to the government the worker's nationality or residency status. That's not the immigrant's wrongdoing, as even FAIR agrees; that's the system's problem that needs to be fixed.

That system allows illegal immigrants to pay into the Social Security fund for the rest of us, which they are not allowed to benefit from.

Talk about ironic, huh? As documented by a myriad of reports, we benefit in terms of Social Security from the money collected from millions of illegal immigrants. Again, that's the system we now have.

■ "They Don't Pay Taxes"

Now that we've touched on the subject of Social Security, which is deducted from workers' paychecks, let's talk taxes in general. The argument heard from some anti-illegal-immigration activists is "they are freeloaders, they use our services and they don't pay any taxes."

Actually, even if they rent, the person they rent from pays property taxes where they live.

Unless they steal everything they wear or consume, they also pay sales taxes, right? Of course they do.

You may argue, yes, but some may cut grass and do menial jobs without paying taxes. That's true. But that's also true about American citizens who are not illegal and may do some of the same work or run cash only businesses.

The fact is, as I found out when I was asked to investigate this on CNN, many companies, whether they are construction builders or manufacturers, deduct taxes from all workers, even if they are undocumented or the employer doesn't know their status, or says they don't know. Again, that's the system.

As for whether illegal immigrants offer America a net loss or net gain, here as well there are two arguments.

According to the Center for Immigration Studies, a think tank that opposes any form of amnesty, "households headed by illegal aliens imposed more than $26.3 billion in costs on the federal government in 2002 and paid only $16 billion in taxes, creating a net fiscal deficit of almost $10.4 billion, or $2,700 per illegal household."

But I interviewed the former state Texas comptroller Carole Strayhorn, who disagreed. In that border state, undocumented immigrants actually pay more into the state coffers than what they receive in services. Don't take my word for it. Listen to what she told me:

She said that undocumented immigrants contributed $17.7 billion to the state economy, while revenues collected from them exceeded what was spent on services by $424.7 million.

Strayhorn found the citizens of Texas were greatly benefiting by having undocumented immigrants, "illegals," pay for their state services. They were creating a revenue surplus. That's right, surplus.

Here's what she told me during my interview with her: "The report finds that the undocumented immigrants in Texas generated more taxes and other revenues than the state spends on them."

So the argument from anti-immigration activists is that illegal immigrants are taking more from us than they are putting in.

And when I asked Comptroller Strayhorn about that, she told me, "You know, it's just not true."

Furthermore, she said the 2005 numbers revealed that without the help of Texas's 1.4 million undocumented immigrants, the state would be worse off. She discovered that the illegal immigrants paid $1.58 billion into the state revenues, which exceeded the $1.16 billion they received in services.

Now, add to that what I mentioned earlier about Social Security and you do get a very different picture than the one presented by anti-immigrant activists. They're forced by their employers to pay into our Social Security fund so that the rest of us can have the money there for our retirement, but they themselves will never be able to collect.

They are subsidizing our retirement benefits, according to a *New York Times* comprehensive report headlined "Illegal Immigrants Are Bolstering Our Social Security System with Billions," to the tune of $7 billion to $9 billion a year.

▉ Taking Jobs

The biggie, though—the top argument in the anti–illegal immigrant arsenal—is that "those illegals are taking our jobs."

And there is no question they do, and take less pay to boot. But let's examine the other side of the economic story: At the height of the immigration debate in the United States, the U.S. economy was solid. And yet we were arguing over whether these "illegals" were coming over here and taking our jobs.

George W. Bush's secretary of commerce, Carlos Gutierrez, whom I interviewed many times, told me flat out "the United States has a need for labor."

He went further; he said during times of economic growth, many of our industries are sustained by even illegal immigrant labor.

▉ The American Dream

Let me tell you what it looks like from the immigrants' perspective. I know because I grew up with it.

The United States is truly the Land of Oz. The hardships experienced by those of us who come to this country dirt poor are well worth the struggle.

When I came to this country, my family lived in *"la casa de las cucarachas."* You probably remember from my earlier comment why we called it that. It was infested with cockroaches, and we couldn't afford an exterminator, so we made do with bug spray, a lot of swatting, and we tried to keep it as clean as we could, though it seemed an unwinnable battle.

The home, I later learned, was in the Miami ghetto known as Liberty City. There, I shared two bedrooms with my mom and dad, my brother, my aunt, uncle, and two cousins. Eventually, we moved into an apartment in Hialeah, an immigrant enclave filled with factories that resembled H. L. Mencken's description of Pittsburgh during the turn of the century, "the libido of the ugly."

But you know what? To me, it was and still is the most beautiful place on Earth. And I was the happiest kid in the world. I didn't know I was poor. I really didn't. I was living in America. And I believed my parents when they told me that in America, all things were possible. To me, America really was that beacon on the hill that Ronald Reagan used to talk about. They believed it. And I did, too. Still do.

They used this *libertad* word that I didn't really understand because I was only four or five years old. That bigger concept of "freedom," and what it means to have it, didn't make a lot of sense. But I knew we were lucky to have what we had, and to have the chance to become even more if we *worked hard*. That is what my parents taught me, and that's what immigrants come here believing. And they tend to not take it for granted.

When I went away to college on a football scholarship to Minnesota, I told everybody I was rich. I wasn't lying to them. I was lying to myself, I guess. I was poor, poverty-level poor by definition. I just didn't know it. My parents weren't on welfare, they never collected unemployment, they rarely asked for anything. Eventually, we even owned our own small home in Hialeah, where my parents still reside. And they even took me out to eat at Burger King. I can still taste that grape soda and that hamburger. Dining out with my family once a month was for me an enormous treat. Are you kidding me? I was doing fantastic!

My parents would save up enough money every week so that we could do that. Sometimes we would switch it up and visit McDonald's. God, I loved their fries, so different from the beans and rice we were used to having at home. Or as my brother called it, *potash*, an anglicized version of *potaje*, which is what you call mixed beans and rice in Spanish. It is all we could afford, night in and night out.

Let's see, we had a house, an old Packard, and we had enough money to eat at McDonald's or Burger King once a month. That made us, in my eyes, wealthy people. And nobody could ever tell me differently.

After I grew up I looked back and realized we weren't wealthy. We were actually below the poverty level, with a combined family income of just over $6,000 in the late 1960s. But it didn't seem to matter what was in our bank account; what mattered was in our hearts. My parents truly loved me and my brothers and would often go to bed hungry to ensure our satisfaction. That's what I learned from them that I'm passing on to my own kids. I wish I could do it, as well. But how can I? They had nothing and gave us everything. Now I have so much, it embarrasses me to think about it comparatively. The immigrant experience, the ideals, occurs only once, but is hopefully passed on from generation to generation. I'm trying.

Recruitment

The immigrant ideal of America is made even greater when it comes with a guaranteed job. And that is exactly what's happened in America, with some companies being accused of sending recruiters into Mexico to find suitable workers by the hundreds. There is pending litigation against several U.S. companies for doing just that.

But through investigating immigration patterns and workers in America, I have found that more often than not the recruitment occurs within families.

Here's how it works: Let's say Pepe works for Company XYZ. One day, his American employer says to Pepe, "We could sure use a few more people. Do you have an aunt or any family members who might be interested in a job as well?"

Pepe says, "Yeah, but I have to get them over here."

The supervisor says, "That's great, because you know what? We could really use them."

It sounds like just a conversation, but essentially what that supervisor is saying to Pepe is, "If you can get your family over here, they've got jobs."

So Pepe calls his sister in Guadalajara, and before you know it, Luisa is now in the United States and working.

And remember, when Luisa gets here she gets a tax ID number. What that tax ID number gives them is not the right to be in the United States legally, but ostensibly the right to work in the United States legally.

So you've got corporate America telling immigrants, "Come to the United States and we'll give you a job." And you've got the federal government saying, "When you get here, you'll be able to work legally because we're going to give your boss a tax ID number so that we can garnish your wages and make sure you pay taxes."

Does it happen?

I went to Dalton, Georgia, to find out what impact the undocumented immigrants flooding the town have made. I visited the schools, the local businesses, and, of course, the chamber of commerce, and came away quite surprised.

They took me through the history of the carpet manufacturing business, and here's what they said.

"What we have here in Dalton right now are the original workers who came in to the carpet mill industry during the boom after World War II. They came as poor and unemployed Appalachians. The people came down because they needed jobs, and they did a fabulous job.

"Those people who were the pioneers of the carpet industry in the United States in Dalton, Georgia, are now in their sixties and seventies and eighties and are leaving the mills.

"We found ourselves with a need for labor. And meanwhile the demand for carpet was increasing worldwide, making Dalton, Georgia, into 'the carpet capital of the world.'

"So we obviously tried to recruit their sons and daughters and the people from that area of the United States—the tristate area of the Carolinas, Tennessee, and Georgia. We weren't able to get anybody. What we found was that most of the people didn't want to travel in their moms' and dads' footsteps. They wanted to go to the big city. They wanted to go to Atlanta and Nashville."

The only way to keep up with the demand brought on by the housing boom of the '90s, they said, was to increase the labor force. And the only people that they say they were able to hire for these jobs were immigrants. So suddenly you had thousands of immigrants, legal and illegal, pouring into Dalton and creating a community.

So then I drove to a transmission shop and I asked the guy there, "What's it like to deal with the people in this town?"

He said, "Mr. Sanchez, let me tell you something. These people pay on time, they show up when you want them. If you are fixing up their car and you tell them it's going to cost so much, they'll be here with a check a half hour before you show up with the work. There's no need to call them. There's no need to follow up. They are responsible. They're consistent. And, frankly, they make fantastic customers."

Then I went to the elementary school, where I was told most immigrant students were learning English almost immediately after being placed in classrooms. Then they introduced me to their valedictorian, an immigrant from Mexico whose parents were called by the principal so I could interview them in Spanish.

Time and time again, as I went around talking to the members of the business community in Dalton, that's the story they told me.

Again, that's not to say the United States doesn't need an immigration reform process that is concrete, that protects our borders, and establishes who should be allowed to stay and who should not come into the country. But it gives you a sense of why they come here, how they're recruited, what they do when they get here, what the need is, and how it really works out for America.

■ Sheriff Joe

Joe Arpaio is the sheriff of Maricopa County, Arizona, which is essentially Phoenix.

Joe Arpaio is someone who in the past reportedly didn't even believe it was the job of local officials to arrest immigrants or to handle immigration matters. That's what he once told the columnist and my CNN contributor colleague Ruben Navarrette. He said local law enforcement is not supposed to be going out there and arresting illegal immigrants because that's the job of the federal government.

And then, suddenly, Joe Arpaio gets real popular, by coming down hard on illegal immigrants. Out of nowhere, Joe Arpaio becomes "America's sheriff," the most fervent anti–illegal immigrant law enforcer in the United States. He prides himself on it. And guess what? To some, he becomes a hero.

Joe Arpaio is not a federal law enforcement officer. His mandate does not include immigration. But despite what the federal government tells him, he insists that his responsibilities include cracking down on anyone who "looks like they might be an illegal immigrant."

The Constitution be damned? Arpaio says that all he needs for probable cause is a look and a chat. He can tell an illegal immigrant, he said to me, by the way they dress and talk.

That's what he revealed, to the shock of people watching all over the country, when he came on my show. And then the assistant secretary of homeland security came on with me to say the feds didn't want Joe Arpaio's kind of help. And, in short, they wished he would stop.

So I invited Arpaio back, and he told me, basically, he didn't care.

"Like Bull Connor in the 1960s," I told him, "you're going to sit there and tell the feds you don't care what they say, you're going to do it your way and you're going to do it when you want to do it?"

He said, "They don't tell me how to do my job enforcing state laws. I worked twenty-five years as a top Justice Department drug enforcement official. I think I know the federal law and how to operate under the federal blanket. So . . ."

"All right," I jumped in. "Well, for the record, they're saying you don't and they're saying you're violating it."

He was defiant. "Then come on after me, if he thinks I'm violating any of the federal laws!"

It's a tough stand, by a tough man. Or is it?

As my friend Ruben Navarrette from the *San Diego Union-Tribune* came on a little later to explain, it was a relatively new position for Joe Arpaio. As recently as the 1990s, Navarrette said, Arpaio "wanted nothing at all to do with immigration enforcement. He believed, like a majority, like hundreds of police and sheriffs around the country, that this was the job of federal law enforcement officers and they ought not to punt it off to local cops. He said so."

So why the switch? Navarrette pinned it on a single incident.

"In 2005, he got in trouble with the nativists because, in an incident that occurred, he seemed to take the side of illegal immigrants," Navarrette explained. "There was a case of a twenty-four-year-old army reservist who had pulled over illegal immigrants, held them at gunpoint. Arpaio went ballistic on the reservist, said, 'You can't just do that, and make comments about how being illegal in the country— being an illegal immigrant isn't a crime.' And he was right about that.

"The nativists beat him up, and for the last four years, you know, he's acted like a whipped dog. He's learned his lesson, and now he panders to that right-wing element."

His motives don't really matter. His methods do.

A lot of people don't get that. In fact, when I did that story about Joe Arpaio, I looked down at my Twitter Board during a commercial, and I realized that a lot of the people were saying, "Hey, wait a minute. Arpaio is doing what's right. He's a lawman and he's stopping these people who've broken the law."

What those folks were missing was that in the process of arresting illegal immigrants, he may be violating the rights of citizens, people who are here legally. That's why we have rules against unreasonable search and seizure established by the Constitution. That's why the police are supposed to have probable cause. Because we don't expect to live in a country where you can be going about your business and a cop can stop you, detain you, question you, because he didn't like the way you looked.

The issue with Arpaio is not illegal immigration; the issue is him sending his men out into the streets to roust whoever they please—maybe even you.

That smacks against every principle of police procedure that's been in place for something like forty years in this country. He's saying that probable cause doesn't matter.

So, when I saw that people at home and on Twitter weren't catching that, I brought it up again. In fact, I read a tweet from someone suggesting I should leave Sheriff Joe alone, and stopped in the middle of my newscast to address it and refocus the issue. It's not about arresting "illegals," it's about upholding our Constitution.

But how could I make that point more concrete? It didn't really matter what I think, what matters is what Arpaio thinks—so I questioned him further. Here's what I asked him.

"Now," I said, "we come back to the same question, about how you know that they were illegal if you didn't use a method of probable cause that we are not supposed to use in this country." I continued, "There are twenty-five years of laws and standards used by police departments where they're real careful about probable cause so we don't create a Gestapo environment in this country."

He shot back, "We're using the same criteria as the U.S. Border Patrol does (with) everybody," he said, "arresting thousands of people who come into this country and that's under homeland security."

He was comparing himself to federal law enforcement officials, who have a different mandate and work in a different venue. So I pressed him on this.

"But the U.S. Border Patrol is on the border," I said. "You are nowhere near the border."

"Well . . . " He hesitated.

"You're literally going into people's neighborhoods and into schools," I said. "This weekend, you went into a car wash to essentially decide for yourself who was here illegally or not illegally. And the feds are saying they don't want you doing that."

Arpaio stuck to his guns in sticking it to the feds. But then in a later interview I got an answer I didn't expect, even from Arpaio. It was an admission of sorts that seemed shocking in its brazenness.

He told me it's his right to arrest "illegals," just for being in the country illegally, so I wondered how he knows they are illegal. Here's how that went:

"You just said you detain people who haven't committed a crime—how do you prove they're not illegal?"

"It has to do with their conduct, what type of clothes they're wearing, their speech, they admit it, and they may have phony IDs. A lot of variables are involved."

I couldn't believe what I had just heard! "You judge people and arrest them based on their speech and the clothes they're wearing, sir?"

He tried to walk it back. "No, when they're in the vehicle with someone who has committed a crime. We have the right to talk to those people. When they admit that they are here illegally we take action . . . the federal law specifies the speech, the clothes, the environment, the erratic behavior. It's right in the law."

Actually, it's not. In fact, what he's describing is the arguable mandate of a federal law enforcement official and certainly not a local sheriff. The idea that a person can be detained and arrested for their speech and/or the clothes they're wearing smacks against every precept of what the Fourth Amendment of the Bill of Rights which guarantees us against, unwarranted search and seizure. Again, it's not in defense of undocumented immigrants that the law was written, it's in defense of legal residents and American citizens who are repeatedly stopped and harassed by Arpaio, because of what he presumes about their speech or their clothing. In other words, that could be you.

> Arpaio is a product of wild west rule, same with jon
> kyl and hayworth, they all from the same breeder.
> Crazyarizona.

> I think he's similar to what you said he was: "Bull
> Connor."

In late April, Arizona governor Jan Brewer signed into law Senate Bill 1070 as fifteen hundred people outside the capitol protested against it. It might just as well have been called the Joe Arpaio law because it seemed to give credence to what the Maricopa sheriff was telling me and the Justice Department he had a right to do.

The law actually said that police could arrest illegal immigrants after any "lawful contact." What did that mean? I asked that question during my show immediately upon reading the bill. Did that mean that police could lawfully stop anybody and ask them if they were in the country illegally? It did not seem clear.

But then the law, which seemed well intentioned enough as a way of curbing illegal immigration in response to what the federal government had failed to do, became even less clear. Here's how that happened. As we were broadcasting the governor's historic signing and subsequent news conference, I heard a reporter ask, "How do you know what an illegal immigrant looks like?" I thought for sure Governor Brewer would dust off the question and move on. But instead she said she didn't know what they looked like but was sure that the "AZ POST," state police board would put out a "description."

A "description," I immediately asked on the air as I heard the answer played back by my staff to make sure I heard her correctly. Had the governor just put the state police board in a position of putting out a description of what an illegal looks like?

It's what I asked Lyle Mann, the executive director of the Arizona police board, who supported the law; but seemed to wish the governor had not said what she did. He admitted to me that if he answered my question about putting out a "description" of what illegal immigrants looked like, he'd have to be critical of his own governor. Enough said. I got it and so did you.

In the weeks that followed, two Arizona police chiefs, the mayor of Phoenix and several high-ranking officers told me they were uncomfortable with the letter if not the spirit of the new law. And by early May, the law was revised and re-signed by the governor. The wording "lawful contact" was changed to "lawful stop" seemingly to imply the suspected illegal immigrant would have to be in the commission of a crime or some suspected unlawful activity before they could be asked about their legal status, but it may be up to the courts to actually figure it out.

Regardless, Arizona had done what few expected could be done during an election year. It had seemingly pushed congress and the Obama administration to push for what Americans on both sides of immigration divide appeared to be screaming for; a federal comprehensive immigration reform legislation. It may not have been artful, as its critics charged. And it may be proven yet to be unconstitutional, but at least Arizona had gotten the feds to own up to their responsibility. Getting it passed? Now that would be another thing altogether. And while they debated, Arizona was losing millions in tourism and convention business monthly.

▌Legalization

It's exactly what the previous administration had attempted. George W. Bush, John McCain and Ted Kennedy had earnestly tried to change the system and were punished for it with a backlash when they tried to give 12.5 million undocumented immigrants a chance to earn their citizenship. They were going to make them prove they had been here for at least a year or more, pay a fine of thousands of dollars, go through an extensive criminal background check, go back to their country for a year, and get back at the end of the line and apply to be readmitted. The aim of comprehensive immigration reform was to make undocumented immigrants sacrifice to become citizens.

What was the reaction from undocumented immigrants? "Where do I sign up?" That's what they told me when I set out to do a story on whether they would embrace the reform. I left the CNN Center and drove to Buford Avenue outside Atlanta, which has become a Central American enclave.

"¿Estarían dispuestos a hacer esto? Are you willing to pay the fine, leave the country, prove you've been here without committing a felony, and so on?" I asked.

All I got was, "Sí," "sí," and "Sí, ¡absolutamente!" It would be their dream come true, they told me.

But they never got the chance.

Not enough public support was able to overcome the coalition of conservatives on both sides who worked to squash it, because they said it was "amnesty." One word, repeated probably a thousand times a day by every conservative broadcaster and talk-show host in the country, killed the reform. That word was used again and again, like a bludgeoning tool. No nuance, no comprehension. Just "illegal" and "amnesty" was all they needed to scare away any support from Republicans who were more afraid of losing votes than doing what seemed to make sense. George W. Bush and John McCain, who put their reputations on the line by publicly supporting the bill, were stampeded by the right wing of their party.

It's funny. First the argument is "they're illegal." And then when somebody says, "Okay, let's see if we can come up with a plan where we can decide how to screen some of them to see if we can make them legal," then somebody yells out we can't because that would be "amnesty."

Many call that a circular argument.

The Dream Act

Some of the people hurt the most by these attitudes are children.

How?

Here's the way I described it on my show.

"I want you to think back to when you were a seventeen-year-old kid, about to graduate from high school. The rest of your life is ahead of you, so you think to yourself. And then someone says, 'Hey, I know you sound American, feel American, and think of yourself as a regular American kid, after you have grown up in the United States. You speak English just like the rest of us. You barely speak Spanish or any other language from where maybe your family came from. But guess what. Get out!'" That's what the deported youth told me.

As I pointed out, when I had the director and one of the subjects of a documentary called *Papers* on my show, that is what is happening to thousands of kids in this country brought here as babies by their parents.

Are they illegal immigrants? Yeah.

The young man I spoke with, Walter Lara, had been here since he was three years old. He had so many honors classes and Advanced Placement courses and such great grades that he had a GPA of 4.7. He had done a thousand hours of community service.

Then, when he was just about to graduate from high school, he got notified by immigration officials that he was going to be deported. Here's a kid who thought of himself as American, and wanted nothing more than to go on to college and become a productive member of society.

And his parents? They paid their taxes, worked hard, had never committed a crime. And after a decade and a half of being here, they were going to be kicked out. And so was Walter.

Was that the right thing to do? Legally, maybe yes. Morally, some of you say no. You ask what are we gaining, as a country, by throwing out kids like this? Imagine what a kid with that many accolades, that kind of mind, could contribute.

> Rick, those immigrant kids are true American patriots and role models more so than most apathetic real citizens.

> if they r undocumented they should not be allowed 2 stay. Illegal is still illegal.

Legislation has been introduced on Capitol Hill to allow kids like Walter to stay—twice—but still hadn't passed as this was being written.

It will place American citizens in direct competition with illegal aliens for scarce slots in freshman classes at state colleges and universities while awarding the illegal alien students with an amnesty.

■ A Supreme Difference

When Sonia Sotomayor was nominated for the Supreme Court, I went to Miami to do a story about it. I mean, what a moment! For the first time in the history of the United States, it looked like we were going to get a "wise Latina woman" as a member of the highest court in the land, so I decided to find out what a wise Latina woman was.

I brought together four dazzlingly intelligent and attractive women: a federal prosecutor, a very successful defense attorney, a brilliant activist, and a wonderfully talented and passionate broadcaster from a Spanish-language TV station. We met at my mother's house, the house where I grew up. And I asked my mother to make *cafecito*, and set out some traditional Cuban *pastelitos*, and we gathered around the table to talk about Sonia Sotomayor and about things that affect the United States.

It was wonderful. And then, toward the end of the conversation, I said, "You know what? I'm going to ask my mom [who was in the kitchen making Cuban coffee for us] a couple of questions." So I took it upon myself to ask my mom, and she expressed her very sincere opinion that it made her proud to know that a Hispanic female was about to become a member of the Supreme Court. She spoke from the heart, in the only language she knows—Spanish. So I did a simultaneous translation, and I put that in my report, and it was broadcast all over America.

■ Backlash

Well, some people were outraged. People from all over started sending me e-mails insulting my mother. It was very painful. "Why does your mother not speak English? How long has your mother been in this country now?" And "I can't believe she doesn't speak English. I can't believe you would put her on TV. She sounded like an idiot."

And I talked to my executive producer, and I said, "You know, I'm going to address this."

So on the air, right in the middle of my newscast, I said I wanted to answer some of those comments. I said: "My mom can't express herself in English, because I can," I said. "She isn't accomplished or wealthy, because I am. My mom missed meals when I was growing up so that I could eat.

"You see, my mom didn't bring me to America so she could become successful or educated. She brought me to America so I could become successful and educated. She couldn't go to night school to learn English, because she spent ten to twelve hours a day in a factory sewing leather shoes while my dad washed dishes and cleared tables at Miami Beach hotels.

"Their story is the story of millions of immigrants who came to America, maybe even the story of your ancestors. They struggled, went without, and even sacrificed their own betterment, so that we could thrive."

My mother, and the millions of immigrants before her who brought their children to America, resolved to sacrifice for their children. Let me explain what I mean when I say that her not being able to learn English or understand the American culture turned into a blessing for me and my brothers.

When I was growing up, it was my responsibility when the phone rang to see if my mother double-clutched. If she said, "Wet wong momeh" (translation: wait one moment), that was a cue for me or my brother to run over to the phone and start speaking English with either an accountant, a lawyer, a representative of the bank, my dad's boss, or anybody who was calling to do business with my parents. Those three words—translated: "wait one moment"—meant she needed us to conduct the family business.

My brother and I ended up doing everything from accounting to law on the phone, and negotiating things most twelve-year-olds would never imagine having to have conversations about. It made us wise beyond our years. You grow up fast. But you grow up surrounded by love, trust, and unity.

Tongue-Tied

Remember Mrs. McCalvane, my first-grade teacher who thought I was retarded because I didn't speak English? Mae M. Walters Elementary School was two blocks from my house. Mrs. McCalvane, an elderly genteel woman with a Southern accent, was seemingly as terrified of me as I was of her.

I was in a new country, in the back of a classroom, wondering what strange people these were and what strange sounds they made. I was one of the first off the boat, so to speak, so there were no others like me in my class.

I failed first grade and my mom got the note from Mrs. McCalvane spelling out my problem: "Ricardo Sanchez has a learning deficiency and may suffer from a mild retardation." She suggested to my parents that they take me out of school, because I might not be able to adapt in a "normal school."

Mrs. McCalvane's evaluation was wrong. But she may have done me a huge favor. She seemed to make me want to prove her wrong. I went on to win every award that Mae M. Walters Elementary School had to offer.

On graduation day at Mae M. Walters Elementary School, seven years after Mrs. McCalvane's pronouncement, I was awarded the Junior American Citizen award, the presidential award, the best athlete award, the American Legion award, and the student "most likely to succeed."

I didn't expect my parents to be there, because in those days you couldn't exactly take a day off from factory work without risking losing your spot on the production line.

I didn't expect my dad to miss work for my graduation and awards assembly and he didn't. But apparently someone had tipped off my mom. And she found a way to get off work.

There in the back of the room, discreetly tucked into a corner for fear of embarrassing herself or me because of her lack of English skills, was the woman who had brought me to America. I held up the American Legion award over my head and found my mom's eyes looking back at me. I beamed. She smiled, but a tear fell down her cheek.

Pride. Sacrifice. Accomplishment. The greatness of America was captured in that one moment.

ACKNOWLEDGMENTS

It's not easy to believe in someone who doesn't make things easy. I owe this book to those who've done just that, despite my penchant for relentlessly challenging conventional wisdom.

This is for all of us nonconformists, who believe that things don't need to be the way they are, just because they are. Brazen are those who follow nonconformity, despite the heat it attracts.

I begin by acknowledging my executive producer, Angie Massie; news supervisor, Jim Lemay; my field producer, Michael Heard; and my weekend producer, Tenisha Abernathy. I also want to thank my atypical *Rick's List* staff: Michael Heard, Gary Daughters, Chris Hall, Janelle Griffin, Barb Vargas, Charles Ashe, Dave Johnson, Johnny Hutchens, Jim Reed, Pam Wessman, Anjie Taylor, Alicia Eakin, Reid Binion, Andreas Preuss and Stefanie Jewett.

I want to give a special thanks to CNN's suits for allowing me to go against the grain: Jon Klein, Rick Davis, Phil Kent, Jim Walton, Bart Feder and Janelle Rodriguez. I also want to thank the agent with the toughest rep job in the country, Ken Lindner.

Now to what is most important in my life: my mom and dad, who had nothing and gave me everything, and my brothers, Chuck and Rudy, who've believed in me through triumphs and struggles.

When you're an immigrant from Miami who's taken an unconventional path through a difficult career in journalism, you need a partner to write a book who understands the meaning of unconventional. This book could not have been written without the writing assistance and cooperation of veteran journalist and dear friend Carlos Harrison. I also want to thank Ray Garcia and Mark Chait from Penguin Group (USA) Inc. for guiding me through unknown territory.

To my best friend, Mark Darrow, who inspired me to write— thanks for being there.

Now comes the tough part—the part that makes me sad. Writing is an all-consuming experience that causes as much heartache as joy, and expends more feelings, mood changes and hours of concentration than most fathers and husbands have in a day.

The sacrifice was not mine; it was my family's time that was taken away. I have been blessed to have by my side throughout the writing of this book my beautiful wife, Suzanne, to whom I will be eternally grateful, not to mention forever in love!

For all the missed dinners and outings, I'm sorry. To my eldest, Ricky, who tells me he now goes by Rick: your leadership skills and college successes make me so proud. To Robby, my teenage "walking encyclopedia" son: Your mind and theatrical talent leave me in awe.

Then there are our two little ones. To Remington: Now finally we can throw the football every day after work—what an arm you have. And to my baby girl, Savannah, tough, smart, beautiful and loving, though slightly impatient—you're about to be rewarded. Yes, we will be getting the puppy I promised!

I love you all.